What to Tell
Your Children About Sex

Also prepared by The Child Study Association of America

CHILDREN AND THE THREAT OF NUCLEAR WAR

What to Tell
Your Children About Sex

Prepared by
The Child Study Association of America

Foreword by MILTON I. LEVINE, M.D.

DUELL, SLOAN AND PEARCE

New York

First edition

Affiliate of
MEREDITH PRESS
Des Moines & New York

Library of Congress Catalogue Card Number: 64-24488

MANUFACTURED IN THE UNITED STATES OF AMERICA FOR MEREDITH PRESS

VAN REES PRESS • NEW YORK

FOREWORD

By Milton I. Levine, M.D.

Sooner or later every parent finds himself face to face with the problem of sex education. We try to answer the many questions of the growing child—but when the questions deal with sex, reproduction, and the feelings of the adolescent, we find ourselves bewildered.

Most modern parents realize the almost vital importance of adequate sex education. They are aware of its influence on the child's normal development, his later adjustment to the opposite sex, and his ultimate happiness. But these same parents find themselves overpowered not only by the complexity of the problem, but also because they feel strangely uncomfortable, hesitant and inhibited when speaking of sex. Unfortunately, most of us are products of a generation in which sex talk was taboo. As a result, we lack the knowledge to answer adequately questions relating to sex, and those of us who have the knowledge all too often lack the vocabulary.

But the problems that confront the parent of a growing child are complicated, and often require more than personal experience. We may have some background and even some knowledge as to when and how to describe differences in sex and the process of reproduction. But other more difficult questions arise. What about masturbation? What about books on sex education? What about the child who asks no questions concerning sex? What about nudity before our children? How can we direct the sex urges of our adolescents? What about necking and petting? What about crushes?

These are but a few of the questions arising throughout the development of the child. Every parent needs knowledge and understanding of a child's sex conduct, and the better we are equipped to guide our children, the greater the insurance for future adjustment and happiness.

It follows that a parent has need of a dependable source of information on this difficult subject. This book presents a clear, wholesome, and intelligent approach to the problems of sex education. Within its pages the various problems of sex and reproduction are discussed—and answers are presented. It should be an invaluable aid to the modern parent who desires to give his child an adequate background and a sound and healthy attitude toward the whole subject of sex.

CONTENTS

INTRODUCTION

This book is for parents who want to know how to tell their children about sex.

It is written simply and plainly, in question-and-answer form, under the direction of The Child Study Association of America, one of the oldest organizations in the country concerned with building sound parent-child relationships.

It is also designed as a handy reference manual. Each stage of child development, from infancy through adolescence, is covered in a separate section. And within each section there is information on children's questions and on questions parents ask about their youngsters' sexual growth.

The book is as definite as it can be. It should be noted, however, that growth patterns may vary widely from person to person. In using the book, do not expect a child to fit all descriptions exactly in each age group. He may develop at a faster or slower rate or in a different way and still be a fine, happy child. Try instead to view the information as a general outline and apply it to the child as his own growth seems to require it.

One big point: This is a book for fathers as well as mothers. All the jokes about Dad's clumsiness in giving sex instructions are no joke. Boys and girls need his guidance and example as a male, right from the start.

A small point: Don't be put off by the general use of the personal pronouns "he," "him," "his." They are used to mean both boys and girls.

One final point: Over-all, this book is designed to help you give your children the knowledge—and the encouragement—that will help them to become healthy, normal adults with a wholesome, comfortable feeling for sex and a capacity to love.

1 "WHAT IS SEX?"

It is a part of growth,
part of personality,
part of love.
Living comfortably and
familiarly with it
is a mark of the mature adult.

ITS PART IN EMOTIONAL GROWTH

Basically, the word "sex" means "being male or female." Beyond that it is the differences in body structure that separate male from female. It also means "sex appeal," the attraction that draws male and female together. And it applies to intercourse, pregnancy, and childbirth—the processes that depend on and result from these human relationships.

Like most definitions, these tell us much without telling enough. They show sexuality to be one of the basic facts of life on earth—a natural state of balance that permits human existence and assures that it will continue. And they indicate its humanness—but not its humanity. They give no sign of the warmth, ardor, and tender regard that are involved in a sexual relationship. They do not show that in human terms sex is a part of love, an expression of the desire to find meaning and worth in another person, to make him (or her) the heart of our kindness and affection, to find in generous feeling the basic happiness of human living.

Neither do they show that for many people in the United States today, sex means worry and embarrassment. It is a puzzle, a problem, uncomfortably accepted and uneasily explained to others.

Why so? Probably there are many answers. Certainly one would seem to be our background—the stern views of our grandparents, and theirs before them, that sex was wickedness and a sin of the flesh. These views have died slowly. Times have changed, of course. The old ways are perhaps losing their power to keep us from expressing ourselves sexually. But they can still make us feel guilty for doing so.

3

There is evidence of confusion and uncertainty in the vastly different attitudes we have toward different parts of our sex life. We like and admire the sexy glamor boys and girls of our movies, TV, and books, and yet we disapprove of youngsters or adults who behave the same way "in real life." We believe in lasting marriages, and yet we have a high divorce rate. We like to think we are wise and up-to-date in our ideas about sex, and yet we are often fumbling, tongue-tied, and untruthful in the way we prepare our youngsters for the sexual side of life. We have too many tots whose natural interest in sex is discouraged. Too many tense little grade-school girls worried about menstruation. Too many adolescents baffled and upset by the surging changes going on within their bodies. Too many emotionally childish adults. Too many parents passing on the mistakes of their own sexual upbringing to the children coming along.

This is not a happy picture, to be sure. But it is not a hopeless one, either. As an expression of the capacity to love, sex is an endless opportunity. Giving love openhandedly and receiving it trustingly are possibilities for everyone who seeks them.

This book covers the various stages of personality development in children from infancy through adolescence. It tries to weave sex (as an aspect of love) into this pattern of growth rather than treat it as a separate problem which can be "handled" with a few wholesome words of advice. For emotional growth comes only by exercising one's full range of feelings, even as physical growth depends on free play of the muscles and mental growth on flexing the imagination. Further, the place where all emotions are first tried on for size and color is the home. And here all elements of life are jumbled together through the swiftly running days; no one can sift out the moment which is exclusively sexual, or separate it from the moments of joy, pride, torment, wonder, grief, or greatness.

Hence, while this book is concerned with sexual development, it would not have readers feel that their success or failure as parents can be measured by what they have done—or failed to do —in the sex education of their children. There is far more to the business—or art—of being a parent than this, and wide variation in the way parents meet the challenge. It would be rash, as well as inaccurate, to say that one is right and all the others wrong.

As a parent, therefore, you will understand that this is not a book of rules, but a guide. Choose from it the information you think is best suited to your home and family, that you think will best encourage the healthy sexual development of your children. Expect to make mistakes. But remember that children are flexible and forgiving as long as your effort is honest, persevering, and hopeful.

2 FIRST QUESTIONS

Very early in life,
children will ask
how they come to be born.
There's no reason for
not telling them.

THE BEGINNING OF SEX FEELINGS

Sex education starts in intangible ways almost at the beginning of a child's life. But at two or three, when he is talking and active enough to take an interest in his own body and those of the people around him, he generally begins to ask specific questions.

This development comes as part of his general interest in the family group and the part each member plays. He begins, in short, to note similarities and differences. Among these, the most obvious will be physical. He will see that Mommy looks different from Daddy in several respects, that little girls are equipped differently than little boys. There is nothing more natural than that he should want to know why.

How much you say and the words you use to say it will, of course, depend on the way the question is raised. Be prepared to handle questions whenever they come up and try not to postpone them. Small children have almost no time sense and "later" is the same as no answer at all. He may have forgotten what he wanted to know by the time you are ready to discuss it. The naturalness will be gone, and you will be trying to stage-manage a situation he is no longer interested in.

"What's that?"

Little children usually ask first about their own genitals. What are they called?

To the little boy, Mother (or Father) might reply: "That's your penis. All little boys and grown-up men have one. Girls and mommies are different. Instead of a penis, they have a special little opening in their bodies."

For the little girl, the answer is simply reversed. The opening, which all girls and women have, is the vagina. Boys have a penis instead. It is reasonable to want to simplify terms, but try to avoid inaccuracies that may create false impressions and have to be corrected later.

"Why doesn't a girl have a penis?"

You may find that your young one has difficulty accepting the basic bodily differences. No matter what you say, your girl—or boy—may decide that everyone should have a penis and that girls have somehow lost theirs. A girl may resent this imagined loss and feel that it is some kind of punishment. A boy may fear losing his. There's no predicting the notions a youngster may get and cling to.

Explain that every girl has a vagina and every boy has a penis, and it is right to be this way. Assure the child that he is as he was meant to be and will never change. (If a little girl seems upset because she doesn't have a penis, it will probably help to reassure her that only women can have babies.)

"Why is Daddy's penis bigger than mine?"

Small boys may be concerned about the size of the father's sex organ compared with their own. But, again, it is best to emphasize the rightness of things as they are. Daddy's penis is bigger because his whole body is bigger. As children grow up, all parts of them become larger. (Daddy's hand, foot, arms, etc. are larger than yours.)

"Where does a baby come from?"

By three or four, a child may begin to wonder where he came from. This may be a growing awareness of himself and an interest in hearing how he fits into the family. Or he may suspect or be puzzled by the fact that another baby is on the way. Or the idea may simply have occurred to him and seem to need an answer.

All you may have to say at this point is that a baby grows inside the mother's body in a special place planned just for that purpose. If that seems to satisfy him, let it go at that. If he seems to want to know more, you can add that the special place is called the womb or uterus, and that while the baby is there a cord from inside her body to his gives him nourishment until he has grown big enough to live in the outside world. Meanwhile, her body keeps him warm and protected.

Quite often a child will take this to mean "in the tummy." And too many parents are content to let it go at that—or even to plant the idea in the first place. Don't be one of them. A plain, honest, explanation of sex is hard enough for young children to grasp. Don't let them be confused by inaccurate terms. Talking about reproduction in terms of "a seed growing inside Mommy" will also give a child some odd and mistaken notions. Many children decide they have been born through the navel. Some think of "seeds" in connection with plants, or swallowing a fruit pit, and assume, as many primitive people do, that birth is part of the digestive process.

"Where does the baby come out?"

This question may follow directly upon the first, or it may not. Usually it comes when the child is ready for it, and your answer need not be volunteered earlier or postponed until later. Tell your child that the baby comes out of a special opening in the mother's body, between her thighs. This serves as an opening into the world from the place where the baby has been growing. The passageway is called the vagina.

Girls—and boys, too—may not always understand that in a woman there are two different openings. You might add, therefore, that just in front of the vagina is an opening, the urethra, for urination.

Occasionally a child will ask to "see the place where I came out." This may sound like natural curiosity, but most parents will realize that it would be unwise to satisfy the wish. You can simply say you'd rather not, but can draw him a picture and tell him whatever he wants to know. Aside from upsetting the child unnecessarily, it would be an invasion of your own personal privacy.

"Does it hurt to have a baby?"

Yes, it may hurt a little while the baby is being born, but after the baby is born the mother is so glad to have him that she soon forgets about any pain she may have felt. Children sometimes wonder about this. And since pain is linked with fear, your answer should be a calm one. Explain that when the baby is ready to be born the uterus helps the process with a pushing motion of its own. The mother feels these muscles working and knows it's time to go to the hospital where a doctor can help, so that everything goes well for mother and baby. Make it clear that going to the hospital does not mean that Mommy is sick, but that she wants extra care for a while.

"Why can't men have babies?"

They aren't meant to. Nature has arranged this for women. Men's bodies have no special place (uterus) where a baby can grow and no passageway to let a baby come into the world. Their part is to help start the baby in the mother's body and to take care of the mother and children later.

"Why do grownups have hair on their bodies?"

We don't know exactly, but pubic hair and hair under the arms are another sign of growing up. So is the hair on Daddy's chest and the whiskers on his face.

"Why do women have breasts?"

Breasts make the milk that feeds little babies. That is the way many mommies feed their children before they learn to use a cup. Little girls get breasts as they grow up; little boys don't.

"Will I have a baby, too?"

Most children ask this, or assume it with a flat statement that they intend to have babies when they grow up. You can agree that they will be parents without going into complicated ideas of marriage or adult love relationships. Simply tell them, "When you grow up you'll get married and have babies." Small boys, of course, should not be allowed to think they can bear babies, but are generally satisfied to know they will be daddies, even before they have thought to ask what a daddy's role is.

FOR THE PARENT

When do sex feelings begin? From the moment of his arrival in the world, your baby is stirred by physical feelings. Their range is not wide. Like everything else about him, his emotional responses are simple, basic, and direct. His small body feels contentment and pleasure at being warm, being cuddled, being fed, or just being. Or, if his needs are not met, his muscles tense, his body quivers with unhappiness, and he cries. Every parent knows this.

What is less well known is that in these ways, even this early in life, the baby begins to learn about what we later call sex. Through his various sensations he begins to know and appreciate himself as a person and thus to know and appreciate others. Naturally, changing these first bodily sensations into the complex emotions of maturity takes many years. All the steps are linked, however, and none is more important than those he takes in his first year, even before he has spoken his first word.

What does baby learn first? Once he has begun to breathe, baby's efforts—and his feelings—are keyed to the satisfaction of his appetite. With his first strong reflex action—sucking—he learns to feed himself at breast or bottle. Above all, this eases his hunger pangs and, of course, keeps him alive. But before long it is also a pleasure. He gurgles and sighs. He is shaken by delicate, small shudders at the delightful feeling of being full after the discomfort of being empty. Often he wants to go on sucking even though it is plain he couldn't hold another drop. Between feedings he sucks on his fingers or a toy.

Through sucking, too, he makes his first contact with another person. This is an important relationship. The way he feels about it will help to shape his later attitudes toward people generally. If, for instance, he is soothingly rocked while feeding he will feel the warmth of human affection and will be encouraged, as he grows up, to love others. By contrast, the baby who is held stiffly and without affection, or who is left alone in his crib most of the time to feed himself, will be less sure that the world is a friendly place in which to live.

Can an unhappy experience at this age do permanent damage? Probably no single everyday experience, happy or unhappy, has a permanent effect. Children do not grow up loving mankind because their bottles are on time or hating it because they are late. But it is true that patterns of feeling start to form very early around the simple events of a baby's life. This does not mean, however, that baby must—or can—be protected from upsets by a rigid and unchanging schedule. What happens is less important than how it happens. Baby doesn't enjoy his bath just because it comes at ten each morning and makes him pink and sweet, but more because he sees your smile and is fondled and talked to. This affection may not in itself guarantee a bright future for the child, but it is a positive value which will help him, as he grows, to meet life openly, kindly, without fear.

Does baby sense my being tense or angry? Yes, he may. He can sense unhappiness as well as happiness insofar as it affects him. Naturally, you won't want to expose him to it as a regular thing, but if you've had a rough day don't be afraid that your mood will harm him.

Why does baby put everything in his mouth? As the months go by, the mouth becomes baby's chief means of testing new elements in his world. Whatever comes to hand is thrust into the mouth to see if it will stir up the feeling sensations he has learned are there. Since he doesn't know enough to choose, many of the items he mouths may be odd and certainly not to your taste. At the same time, he is not likely to agree that he is better off for having an object taken away from him. As far as he is concerned, he has simply been prevented from enjoying himself.

Sucking is a natural activity for infants and need not be a problem if the child is given opportunities and freedom to suck on objects that are safe.

When does sucking stop? Usually when the youngster becomes interested in trying out his surroundings and using his hands in other ways. This is not so much a matter of age as of personality growth. As a child advances to new activities, such as playing with other children or with toys that have a meaning for him (trucks, trains, etc.), he begins to drop more babyish habits. Of course, the process is rarely clean-cut. Few children ever give up sucking all at once and forever. There will be times of tiredness or unhappiness when it seems easier to be a baby again and to return to the comfort of sucking.

Of all baby habits, thumb-sucking seems to bother parents most. It raises the fear that baby's teeth and jaws will be deformed. Since no parent wants that, firm treatment is often used. Many a child has been bound up in elbow splints, swathed in mittens, or smeared with bad-tasting liquids to break him of the sucking habit.

Actually, these harsh cures just don't work. And they aren't necessary. While experts are by no means agreed on the effects of thumb-sucking, studies seem to show that little harm will be done if the youngster has stopped sucking before he gets his second teeth. Even if the first teeth are not quite straight, they tend to right themselves as thumb-sucking tapers off.

Fussing and nagging about the habit only increases the child's tension and probably prolongs his need to suck. Thumb-sucking in itself is not a sign of disturbance, but if coupled with other signs of not wanting to grow up as the child enters the school years, professional help may be needed. (For suggestions as to how and where to get help, see page 109.)

Is masturbation dangerous? No, not in the sense that generations of parents have worried about. It definitely does not lead to ailments or injuries of any kind and is, in fact, coming to be regarded as a normal part of sexual development.

Masturbation begins in young children as the result of a natural interest in touching and finding out about their bodies. They soon discover that there is a pleasant, enjoyable feeling to be had from touching or rubbing the genitals, and so they do it, usually to the great distress of their parents.

For the most part, such worry is needless. Masturbation just does not cause insanity, skin blemishes, blindness, poor sexual adjustment in adult life, or any of the other troubles parents frighten themselves with. What can happen, however, is that a child may develop unhealthy feelings of anxiety and guilt, if he has been constantly scolded or punished for masturbating. This is a real threat to mental health; masturbation in itself is not. If your child seems to be taking pleasure in many other interests, the masturbating can be ignored.

Most children, even if they have not been directly scolded or threatened, seem to sense quite early that masturbation is something that is not generally accepted. They sense this because they notice it is not done openly or publicly by older children or by adults. If your child is himself bothered by his masturbation, help him in any way you can to find other satisfactions. His life may be too inactive, his rest periods too long. He may need to be occupied in new ways, or to have more time and affection from his parents. If masturbation continues to interfere with the widening of his interests and activities, it might be well to get professional help.

In any event, avoid harsh criticism or frightening threats. And don't try to "talk it out," even sympathetically. Usually, a child doesn't want to talk about masturbation—and shouldn't be forced to. If he feels that you enjoy him and like to do things with him, he will sense your support and understanding.

When does sexual curiosity begin? Any time from the age of one and a half on. Even as the child discovered his—or her—fingers and toes, so he will discover his genitals (the external sex organs) and want to touch and inspect them. This is quite normal, completely innocent, and to be expected. At the same time he is likely to become interested in urination and bowel movements. He will want to see the size of his stools, may want to feel them, and may not even mind soiled clothing. He will also be curious about the toilet habits of other children.

For adults with feelings of privacy about bathroom matters, the blunt and primitive interests of the child may be trying. Yet this, too, is a chance to give him a comfortable, healthy pattern of feeling about himself. The attitude toward physical functions that you pass on to him will be the basis for his feeling of pride and rightness—or shame and worry—about the way his body works.

What about toilet training? Many of your child's feelings about himself will be formed as you undertake the unavoidable task of toilet training. As with most learning, your success will depend upon your ability to see the process from the child's point of view. To you, toilet training may be a necessity—or may stem simply from the feeling that you can't face one more diaper change. To him it is a forward step not easily taken. It is a difficult physical process to bring the untrained muscles of bowel and bladder under control, and one that cannot be mastered until the nervous system is mature enough to take over. Since the child doesn't know or care that he's being messy, it also means giving up a familiar pleasure in order to gain your approval.

His impulse to please the people he loves is strong. Yet his abilities may not equal his intentions. Bear with him. Make your training gentle and gradual. Help him to understand what you want him to do and avoid showing displeasure when he fails. Give him the patience and warm approval he needs to feel that the struggle is worth while.

It would be too bad if during this training he gets the feeling from you that any part of him is bad or dirty. Long before he understands words he will be sensitive to looks, gestures, and tones of voice. To suggest that he is not the cozy, neat little person he feels himself to be will raise doubt, confusion, and anxiety in him. This is especially important because he may confuse his toilet functions with his sex organs.

When is he ready to start? Usually children are ready to start learning bladder control when they can hold their urine for about two hours during the day. This happens with most children between fifteen months and two years. Bowel training is a more complicated affair and should start when your child is ready for it.

(Control of elimination involves a whole set of muscles—called sphincters—and the child must be mature enough to grasp what is expected of him.) His muscles must be developed to the point where they can be consciously controlled at the proper time. On the average, babies are ready to start learning bowel control between one and two years of age. As his eliminations become more regular he will be far better able to co-operate and far more willing. If he can see that he is sharing in his own training, he will take greater pride in his accomplishment and be less likely to slip back into soiling and wetting later on. A relaxed, loving approach will make the child feel that his parents want to help him in his efforts.

What words should I use? Parents often find it hard to give names to the various parts and functions of the body. Sometimes modesty—or false modesty—in their own background leads them to use vague, inaccurate, or polite, meaningless terms. Or sometimes they are content to use the mixed-up baby words of their own childhood.

This is all right, although a child will need to know the proper terms—urine, vagina, penis, etc.—eventually, and it will certainly do no harm to let him know them early. As a matter of fact, they are not easy words to pronounce, and he will need some time to get the hang of them.

One caution: As with practically everything having to do with sex, it's usually best to suggest that the child use his new words only in the home. Each family in a neighborhood usually has its own way of handling sex questions, and your child may be scolded for using proper terms openly. Respect for others' ways of doing things is just another part of the social manners he is already learning.

Should a child see his parents nude? To begin with, at one time or another he probably will. Try to take it in stride.

Nudity embarrasses many adults and may spur them to say something abrupt that leaves the child feeling he shouldn't have asked about it. To be blamed for having natural curiosity gives the child a tingle of guilt. One good way for children to learn about nudity is to allow them to see other children.

Still other grown-ups today make a point of going nude in front of their children, believing that it's best to be natural and that it helps give the young ones a wholesome, matter-of-fact feeling toward the body. Actually, this isn't always so. Seeing the nude bodies of grown-ups often arouses a child's interest in touching, exploring, or fondling. This may start feelings and desires in him that can't be satisfied and that are disturbing in many ways. Some children show this clearly. With others you can't be sure. The best plan is probably a fair amount of privacy for grown-ups—although families will probably have to do what seems most natural.

Should I let my child into the bathroom with me? As a regular thing, no. Surely you are entitled to your privacy, and this is a lesson children can learn quite easily. The toilet habits of an adult can help to give a small child an idea of bodily functions and of the way they are performed. Small boys may be shown how to urinate by Daddy. Once a child's own toilet habits are established, however, there is certainly no need to have him in the bathroom as an observer. If at times he beats on the door and insists on being let in, it usually has something to do with a feeling of being shut out. If the child seems worried by your absences, you can tell him "wait for me—I'll be with you in a minute" before you leave him.

Does it help to use examples of sex in nature? Not with little children. The facts of sex are difficult enough for small minds to understand without mixing in examples from the animal or vege-table kingdom. When a child asks about the structure of his body or about babies, it's human experience he's interested in. To be answered with talk about bees and flowers is confusing—and an evasion of the truth.

With older children who have an accurate fund of knowledge to work from, the habits of other living things have some point.

Should little children know about menstruation? It's not often that little children under four or five will ask about menstruation unless they happen to see evidence of it. If by accident they learn that something "special" is going on with Mommy, they may be troubled by it. Blood usually suggests bodily injury. There is, of course, no need to explain the process itself in any way. Children want only the reassurance that nothing is wrong, that Mommy is not sick. The parents' attitude—particularly the mother's—toward menstruation will be the most important thing here. If it is accepted as a natural part of life, the child will have no reason to do otherwise.

What part does the father play in sex education? Just as big a part as the mother. It is important for the growing child to have a clear view of each sex as a guide to his own behavior as a male or female. Because Mommy's role is the more active one in the baby years, there is a tendency in many families to go on letting her be the dominant parent in the children's lives. Yet small boys need a male to model themselves after, and small girls need one as a contrast to their femininity.

Beyond this, there is the fact that between three and five, children feel a rivalry with one parent for the attentions of the other. They become old enough to see that the mother who has been their first and biggest source of love also loves and belongs to Daddy. Whether boy or girl, the child often struggles with difficult feelings of wanting Mommy for himself and yet wanting Daddy's affection and approval, too. While caught in this conflict, the child may try several solutions. A boy at times will want to "marry Mommy" and resent Daddy, and at other times swing to Daddy's side to gain his love and be like him. Little girls usually reverse the situation, wanting to "marry Daddy" and ignore Mommy, and then wanting, as a girl, to be like Mommy.

At this age your child will begin to identify himself with the parent of his own sex. A boy will think that Daddy is the ideal man, and a girl will want to be just like Mommy. For this reason, it is important for the parent to give the youngster something to pattern himself after. If a parent of the same sex is not close enough to the child to become his ideal, there may be a mixup in the child's mind. Don't be surprised if boys insist on playing with dolls or girls act overly boyish, but if this continues beyond seven or eight, parents might do well to check with a professional counselor.

A child's jealousy may seem cute and amusing to adults, but actually there is no joy in it for the child. Don't underestimate the depth of the emotional pull-and-haul going on, and do what you can to protect the child against the conflict of his sexual feelings. Go easy on romping and roughhouse that involve physical contact; avoid having the child get in bed with you; do not encourage his playing a grown-up role—"Are you my little Daddy?"—which is more than he can handle.

More than this, both parents should try to show their unwavering affection for the child, regardless of sex. For the problem will work itself out if and when the child comes to understand that everyone is meant to be what he is and that the important thing is to have enough love to go around for man and woman, adult and child. In time, a child is generally happy to accept his parents as adults and himself as the young one, and to develop his constructive desire to be more and more like them, rather than to win them for himself.

What are my own feelings about sex? There's no problem about the sex education of young children as far as young children are concerned. To them, sex is simply one more fascinating aspect of life to find out about. They explore and they discover, and the results are neither good nor bad—until some adult tells them so.

And what are our adult standards of good and bad, helpful and harmful? They are pretty much what we absorbed as children and built onto as we grew up. Unfortunately, while each generation seems to learn more than the one before it, old fears and superstitions die slowly. Although we know better, and want to know more, there are ingrained, adult anxieties in most of us that make us uncertain, less-than-able instructors of the young.

The questions parents ask of child-study specialists show that they are baffled and embarrassed by the questions their children ask. Unthinkingly, they place adult moral values of "bad" or "dirty" on what we now know are normal sexual curiosity and experimenting. And they may use fear and punishment to stop it. Many parents, unthinkingly, use fables, vagueness, or untruth in telling about the great facts of conception and birth. Certainly no child ever decided on his own that he was brought by the stork or delivered in the doctor's little black bag.

What this adds up to is that the starting point of any parent's effort to guide his child's sexual development depends on what goes on within himself. Explaining the facts of life—what seems to trouble many parents most—actually is the easiest part of the job. Far more important and far more difficult is being aware of one's own attitudes and feelings. For this is the stuff which sets the tone of a family's day-to-day living and forms the background in which children find the material for their own personalities.

What do I feel about myself? This is the simplest and most basic question you can ask. Love starts with appreciation of, and regard for, oneself. With growth it becomes less selfish and expands to include others. It has many variations. We can love parents, brothers, sisters, friends, sweethearts, husband or wife, children—or impersonal but nonetheless real things like country, liberty, music, the sea, or religion. To love means that the lover finds worth and meaning in the loved one, thereby encouraging love in return. Happiness as a human being comes from full exercise of a full range of emotions in both giving and receiving.

This emotional honesty is one of the major elements of maturity. For it enables a person to respond to the world realistically—as it is, rather than as he might wish it to be. And with clear-sighted realism, it becomes possible to make wise decisions for himself and to achieve personal independence. And with freedom, a person is better able to tap his creative talents, to work hard and well, because he knows and enjoys what he is doing.

Naturally, these developments do not occur in just this way. They act and interact upon each other as we gain the experience— and the courage—to make use of them. Their sum is our degree of personal fulfillment. Most of us, let it be said, fall short of the goal. For incomplete growth in any stage of development is carried forward to the next one, and lacks or failings there to the one after that. The result, as we become mature in years, is often a continued childishness in one or another area of our emotional life. Childishness means just that: underdeveloped, inexperienced feelings which keep us from appreciating people or situations to the fullest. The bossy husband, the pouting, "spoiled" wife, the man or woman who is thoughtless of the feelings of others or careless of his responsibilities, are all obvious examples of immature behavior.

At the same time we become so used to ourselves that we rarely take stock of our own strengths and weaknesses, to see if we really are the person we believe ourselves to be. Yet the way our children are raised is bound, in large part, to be a reflection of our own feelings.

Keeping an honest eye on yourself, noting how you act and react, will make you more alert to your child's needs and better able to guide him helpfully.

What do I think about sex? Adults find it easy to give themselves credit for broad-mindedness, humor, and sensitivity—and to forget how uncomfortable they are when a child spouts four-letter words, how embarrassed when he scratches his genitals in public, how surprised that their rebukes for these actions bring tears and re-sentment.

These examples, of course, are not basic attitudes toward sex, but they are part of the great collection of likes and dislikes that every adult has and that mirror the feelings he has deep down.

Obviously, each person can speak only for himself about sex, and no one can tell another what he should feel. Yet to find effective ways to help children, it is important to know what your starting point is. How much should teen-agers pet? Do you laugh at off-color jokes? How do you feel about menstruation? Do you feel intercourse outside of marriage, or before it, is always bad? How do you react to lurid comics or newspaper stories of marriage scandals? "Right" answers to these questions will not necessarily make you a better guide for your child or make him better adjusted sexually. But understanding that you have a point of view on all of them—and a reason for the point of view—will give you a line on your feelings about the part sex plays in life.

When your child comes to you with a question, he wants the facts. But more than that, he wants to find out what *you* think and feel. He comes to you because he trusts you; if he did not, he would have gone elsewhere. He loves you and wants to be like you. He wants to measure his own feelings against yours.

Externally, he proves this by copying you. Little girls hold dolly to their breast or play at cooking or "dress-up" in faithful imitation of Mommy. Little boys take pride in being Daddy's helper, wearing his hat, or pretending to smoke his pipe.

Internally it happens too. The same imitation is applied to the invisible area of feeling.

Whatever the question, words will not be answer enough unless they tell clearly what you feel, which is to say, what you are.

How can I talk about sex naturally? Advice to "be natural" in talking about sex is often confusing to parents, who do not find it at all easy to be. To talk about a penis or vagina to a child is tough going for many parents.

It all depends on what you mean by being natural. Casual? Controlled? Aloof? Or admitting the emotional content of sex and giving it the importance it rates? It is natural to be offhand about the state of the weather, but rather unnatural to treat sex the same way.

As a matter of fact, you can't. There is a special quality of intimacy, of vigor, of significance about sex that no one escapes. And this is as it should be. For out of this intense feeling comes understanding of people's regard for one another and of the great happiness that lies in deep personal relationships. Even small children can sense this. To pretend that sex is not vital is unconvincing and misleading. Repeated many times, this attitude can stunt or warp a child's personality growth and result in an adult who is confused and made anxious by the honest expression of strong feeling. It results in adults who become gruff and stiff at displays of affection, who take pride in never being moved enough to cry, who are afraid of loving to dance or of laughing at themselves.

How can I make talks with my children go more easily? Giving children basic stability, emotionally and sexually, is the great responsibility—and opportunity—of parents. Other authorities and influences will succeed you in time, and other ideas replace yours, as your young ones learn to place trust in people outside the family. But through the long, exciting years of youth they will rely on you. In you they will sense the urgent pulse of life and love that they must acquire for themselves—and they will ask many times, in many ways, for help in understanding it. Here are five ways to help your child in these talks.

1. Be patient. It is hard to grow up. Even with the best of guidance, children grope and fumble and make frequent false starts before they make forward progress. Don't rush them. Be prepared to have the same questions come up over and over again.

2. Be a good listener. It is very important to know *what* your child is asking for. It may be far less than you think—or more. The three- or four-year-old who wants to know where he "comes from" is not really curious about sexual intercourse or childbirth. More than likely he is concerned with finding out who and what he is, and with strengthening his feelings of belonging to you.

Even as he grows older it is not safe to take his questions too literally. Give him what you think he wants, as straight as you can. But don't be anxious to gush forth with all you know. You'll mow him down. Encourage him, too, to say what *he* thinks is the answer to his question.

Listening, after all, is part of mutual give and take. Keep a clear channel between you and your small questioner to the end that you both understand each other better.

3. Keep your terms simple. As far as possible, use words that have a single meaning. Gear your answers to the child's level of experience and understanding.

4. Be honest and be consistent. This is especially important when husband and wife share the sex education of their youngsters. Try to work out a mutually satisfactory point of view with your husband or wife before presenting it to your children. Knowing generally the age at which one type of question or another may be raised, you can talk over ahead of time the situations you may run into. And if you don't figure them all out beforehand, be sure to check with your partner to let him or her know how you handled a question alone.

This simply helps to cut down confusion. It doesn't hurt for a child to know that his parents may differ, that there is more than one way of looking at things. But, at first, he should not have to choose between two answers to one question.

5. Above all, be yourself. It is not necessary to pretend you are enormously wise and never make mistakes. Sooner or later the child will discover that you're not always right, anyway. It will

help if you know it, too. By being yourself you will be far more real as a person, and it is from reality that children learn most.

It cannot be said often enough that it is your own sensitivity to your child's needs that will be your best guide in answering his questions. Don't expect to be a mind reader. You can't catch every thought that crosses his mind. But by close and interested observation you will get to know him and the background of his queries. And to the degree that you are frank and open with him and express your own views without insisting that he adopt them, you will be giving him a wider range of emotion to take in and develop for himself.

3 YOUR CHILD FROM FIVE TO EIGHT

*The facts of life
are confusing to young minds.
Be patient. Be clear.
Be truthful. And expect
to have these important
questions come up over and
over again.*

THE BASIC PREPARATION

In this period, a child's view of the world is greatly widened. He leaves home for school and, although his family tie is still very strong, he makes new contacts with other people who become important to him. Teachers, schoolmates, the parents of friends and the highly admired policeman at the crossroads all will offer information and points of view that help to shape his outlook on life. He will hear more and see more and do more. He will start going to the movies. He will begin to read books, newspapers, and magazines. TV will become more meaningful to him.

He will also want to know more about sex matters. Probably, because he is still so close to the baby years, he will seem too young to get complete answers to the questions he asks. You may feel a temptation to put him off, to wait till "later." Don't do it. The answers you give him now, added to what you have told him before, will be his basic preparation for the time when sex begins to concern him more personally. It will be easier for both of you if he is comfortable and familiar with the facts of life.

"How does a baby get inside the mother?"

This is a natural follow-up to the first questions children ask about where they came from. As with those earlier questions, your child may be asking for less than you think. Fives and sixes may be content to hear simply that the father must start the baby growing inside the mother.

If he wants to know more, you can explain that a fluid called semen, containing many tiny sperm cells, comes from the father's body. One cell joins an egg cell in the mother's body. The joining of these two cells starts the growth of the baby. (Don't be afraid to let a term like "sperm" go unexplained temporarily. This—and many other words—cannot be simplified without becoming inaccurate. As long as the main point of your answer gets across, the child will accept the "hard words" as facts he will understand later.)

"How do the mother and father cells get together?"

The semen containing the male sperm cells comes out through the father's penis which, when a man is grown, can enter into the mother's vagina. This is called sexual intercourse, or mating.

It is quite certain that your child won't understand this the first time it is explained. He's too inexperienced to picture what you're saying. And too "innocent." However sexy the information may seem to you, it won't seem so to him. As a matter of fact, he may find it rather odd and wonder aloud if you aren't telling him some sort of silly story. In any event, he is likely to consider it just one more of the amazing aspects of the wonderful world he is learning about.

"Is semen the same as urine?"

Since there is only one opening in the penis, many children get the idea that semen and urine are the same. The answer, of course, is no. Semen is a special fluid whose only purpose is to carry the male sperm cells from the testicles, where they are formed, to the outside of the body. Urine, which is a body waste, uses the same passageway through the penis, but it comes from a storage sac called the bladder and never appears at the same time as semen.

"Why doesn't the mother's egg go into the father?"

Because men's and women's bodies are built differently. The father's body has no place in which a baby could grow. The mother's body has a uterus (not the "tummy") which is located at the top of the vagina where a baby can develop and grow. Boys should be made to feel that being a father and supporting a family are just as important as bearing children.

"When do a mother and father mate?"

This may seem like a very personal question, but a child of this age is not interested in all the details. A simple statement such as this will usually suffice: mating is a part of their loving each other and wanting to have children. It is a private and personal experience for which the mother and father choose a time when they are quiet and alone.

"How does the baby breathe inside the mother?"

Baby doesn't need to breathe air through his lungs the way people do after they're born. He gets air (oxygen) from the mother's blood, which reaches him through a tube called the umbilical cord.

"Why do I have a 'belly-button'?"

Some time during this period your youngster will discover his navel and wonder why it's there. This is where the umbilical cord attached you to Mommy's body as you grew inside her. After you were born, it was no longer needed and fell off. The place where it was is your "belly-button" or navel. It serves no purpose now.

"Why does the mother get so big?"

A pregnancy in the family or in the neighborhood often brings up this question. Explain that the baby grows inside the mother until he is big enough to come into the world. The uterus in which he grows is made of muscle and can stretch a great deal to make room for him. Fluid also forms inside the uterus to float the baby and protect him from bumps and jolts. The baby does not get so big that he hurts the mother or can't get out. After the baby is born, the mother becomes her usual size again.

"How big is a baby when he's born?"

Usually about six or seven pounds. Sometimes more, sometimes less. You may add that if a baby arrives much earlier than he should and is very small, he may need special care.

FOR THE PARENT

What does my child learn at this age? From his new friends he learns, gradually, many of the skills and techniques for getting on in a neighborhood, and many of the rules it lives by. His body becomes less babyish. He uses his muscles better, not only in games and play, but, eventually, in writing, drawing pictures, or playing musical instruments. Socially, he is fairly primitive at first. Through being in a group, however, he usually learns that others have rights equal to his. And he gains a sharper sense of the results of "right" and "wrong" behavior as they affect him and his relations with the people he wants to love him. Mentally and emotionally, he works hard to understand the facts of his ever widening world; what is so and why it is so. His sense of time and space improves. The basic "now" of his baby days is enlarged to take in "long ago," "far away," and "next week." He picks up the language, dress, customs, and beliefs of his community and his nation.

This, of course, does not make him the same as everyone else. It merely gives him a background. He is also trying very hard to be an individual. Much of his learning is in making personal choices, discovering his likes and dislikes, and finding out his feelings for himself and for other people. Many of the problems he runs into will be practice for the more difficult tests of adolescence.

What is he like personally? Generally, the child is at a nice age and relatively easy to get along with. He continues to grow, but less rapidly than he did as an infant and without the problems of sexual development that very likely will arise in the teen years. He may be a bit bumptious, but is better organized than he was a year or so ago. He is more inventive. He can occupy himself for longer periods of time with a game or a book.

He may accept rules rather rigidly and spend quite a bit of time arguing about them. He will insist, by seven or eight, that he should be allowed to play ball in the rain because you told him, three days ago, that he should spend more time outside. He will walk past a ringing telephone because you told him to pick up his jacket "before you do anything else."

He is not being stubborn, but literal. This stems from a still somewhat limited, yet very clear, view of what is what. You will do well to take advantage of it by giving him every chance you can to decide things for himself. He's too small to run his own life, of course. He needs firm support and direction where the choices are too hard. He can, however, help pace his own way for making the much more difficult choices that will face him in the years ahead.

For one thing, making choices strengthens his feeling for himself as a person with individual likes and dislikes. It makes him less the creature of someone else's wishes. To the extent that he can see himself clearly in these years, he will be better able to pick his way through the bewildering emotional changes of adolescence.

What is he like sexually? From five or six until puberty children *may seem to forget* about sex. They want naturally to keep themselves covered, but may be interested in the bare bodies or genitals of adults or other children. Sexual questions are less frequent and a child may even object rather strongly to hearing about sex. Their physical drives find satisfaction in various games and hobbies.

There is no exact explanation for these attitudes and, indeed, it's clear that there are inconsistencies in them. Several things, however, seem to contribute to the lessening of sex drives at this age. For one, there is a change in the sex glands. Growth hormones may become more active. There is also the more varied and active life children lead at this time. They are able to do and understand more things and have less need to find bodily pleasure in every experience. They feel a sense of achievement and—although they wouldn't put it this way themselves—of personal development in work and play and in being part of a group of children. The pleasure sensations of the younger ages shift. Hunger becomes appetite. Elimination turns to regular—and modest—toilet habits. Although they still depend on their parents, they are often good at concealing it; their interests seem to center in children their own age or in older boys and girls.

This does not make a youngster an utter blank sexually. Obviously, children vary. Some may shift their interest from sex at one age, some at another, some not at all. Some may go in for childish sex play, such as looking at or touching other children's genitals, or telling dirty jokes. Generally, however, this is a not too well understood period when very few elements are on the surface to be seen or talked about. Don't worry about it and don't try to encourage your child to talk out his thoughts and feelings. Try instead to strengthen him in the areas where he is blossoming. Encourage his self-confidence. Praise his accomplishments. The relationship you build now will be very helpful when it comes time to wrestle through the problems of preadolescence (age nine to thirteen) which are just over the horizon.

When should I explain intercourse and reproduction? Of all the questions about sex this is the one parents find most difficult to answer. For some it is a matter of overcoming embarrassment and awkwardness at mentioning intimate physical aspects of life. For others, even those quite willing to explain, there is the discouraging fact that it is not easy to express such deep personal feelings in language a child can understand.

As always, however, a child will gain from any discussion only the amount he is prepared to take in at that time. Few youngsters in the five-to-eight span will have any idea of complex adult emotional states, anyway. As long as they get the truth, if only a step at a time, they will feel helped, and your fumbling as an educator will not trouble them. Words, after all, are only symbols. There is no reason to expect that you will describe the physical sensations of love any better than you describe air, the taste of water, or how to whistle.

This is no excuse for telling a child, "You wouldn't understand. Wait till you're older." Many parents, in fact, postpone talking about intercourse, thinking that it will be easier "later on," when the child's understanding is more advanced. This does the child no service and actually makes it harder for the parent. A child's understanding advances largely at the rate you help it to. If you shirk one stage of the process he will learn it elsewhere, which may leave you with much to undo by the time you are ready to step in again.

When your child asks about intercourse or reproduction, answer him.

How much information is too much? Having convinced yourself that you can tell your child much does not mean that you have to tell him all. There is, as you know, a great deal of factual and emotional detail about intercourse which need not be discussed with a small child. Within the framework of his questions you can answer clearly and completely. But don't try to go beyond them and offer information that hasn't been asked for. Too much information is bewildering; too much intensity is troubling.

How about books on sex? Under the age of six, books on sex are likely to be more helpful to you than to your child. Not because you know nothing, but because of gaps in your information or easier ways of saying hard things than you have thought of.

Parents frequently don't know as much as they think they do. They are up on cookery and politics, on sports and movies, on a variety of ideas and events outside themselves. Yet many of them are surprisingly unsure even about the structure of their bodies and why their various routine functions work the way they do. For such parents books may help in gaining familiarity and ease with the facts they want to discuss with their children, now and in the future.

Children's books on sex are most useful when read with a parent as a springboard into subjects and questions of interest to the child. This is particularly true of books which help explain the arrival of a new baby in the family. But books alone cannot do the job for you.

Sometimes a group of mothers who are timid or unsure about discussing sex with their children can gain confidence by talking out the problem among themselves. It is also possible to arrange, through parents' organizations or social agencies for an informative film with a discussion led by a doctor or a child guidance counselor.

Is modesty natural? Yes. Somewhat between the ages of three and seven, a child usually begins to want privacy when he goes to the toilet and objects to being seen without his clothes. This is wholesome and natural. It means that he's begun to sense the customs of the world he lives in and is trying to adjust himself to them.

Modesty is a sign of growing up. As you know, the very young child is quite unself-conscious about showing himself nude. But if the child of seven or eight parades himself before parents or other adults, his act can't be considered so simple or natural. Exhibitionism—showing off one's body—beyond the early years is one way in which children tell their parents that they're not wholly at ease about themselves. Paying close attention to what a youngster says and does may uncover the problem which is troubling him, although if the behavior continues, professional help may be needed. (See page 109.)

Should children share a bed or bedroom? A bed or bedroom should not be shared with parents. Children who regularly share a bed make physical contact that may be an invitation to sex play. While some such play goes on in the life of most children without mattering much, there are youngsters who will be upset by the guilt feeling sex activity arouses in them.

If it can be managed, brothers and sisters should have separate rooms by the time they are five years old.

Sharing a bedroom with parents is hardly wise, either. Children aren't always asleep when they seem to be and they may be frightened or have overstimulated concern—even little ones of two or three—if they are aware of the sexual activity of their parents. Even darkness is no protection, since youngsters may be troubled by sounds that are strange to them.

Despite inconvenience, it is worth having separate rooms, especially if the child no longer needs attention at night. After a year of age roll the baby's crib into the living room when you go to bed, or, if the bedroom is used as a nursery, put a day bed in the living room for yourself.

In today's small homes and apartments, privacy can be a real problem unless the family co-operates to give each member some time by himself when needed. Just such a simple rule as knocking on any closed door is a courtesy children should learn to understand—particularly if their own privacy is observed in the same way.

Does sex knowledge invite sex play? Specialists in child behavior agree that when sex information is wisely given by parents a child trusts, there is less likelihood of unwholesome sex experiments. A certain amount of sex play seems to be a normal part of growing up. A child's natural interest in his own body makes him curious about others and, as you know, he learns early the enjoy-able feelings that come from touch. If he feels free to talk about sexual matters, however, he will take them more naturally and may not have to turn to sex play as a safety valve for the worry and concern growing inside him.

What can be done about sex play? Sex play is not uncommon among children between the ages of four and nine or ten. They will disappear into the bathroom with their friends and trade "bad words" or giggle about toilet functions. They may undress to show their buttocks or genitals and touch each other. Sometimes it is more veiled and comes out in games of "doctor" or "hospital." Sometimes it may be a more extreme and intense effort at sexual stimulation.

Remember first that some such sex play is to be expected.

If it is carried on too often, however, so that other play is forgotten, it will cause anxiety in a child, if it is not a sign that anxiety already exists. When children are troubled or secretive about their play, it's usually because they are feeling guilty but don't know how to break the pattern they've set up.

At such times, the parents' help is definitely needed. Keep from making a big to-do about it. The child's own bad conscience is often punishment enough.

What the child needs is firm but friendly decisions made for him, decisions that will take the problem out of his hands. A clearly meant "no" to undressing games or group trips to the bath-room, or too-long, too-quiet play behind closed doors will cut down the opportunities for sex activity. Pay closer attention to the ways the child spends his free time, and suggest other interests for him.

Don't feel called upon to explain your actions. You don't have to be rigid or abrupt. A simple remark that "It's better not" is enough. This is a situation in which your authority is understood and does not need spelling out.

It is not even very helpful to go back over the situation later on. Try, instead, to decide for yourself whether there aren't unsatisfactory elements in the child's life as a whole and see what you can do to improve matters.

Will masturbation become a bad habit? It need not. Masturbation at this period of development is no different and no more dangerous than it was earlier. As a matter of fact, you can expect it to crop up at any time from soon after birth on, among boys and girls, and for pretty much the same reasons: for bodily pleasure and the relief of sexual tensions.

Again, remember that some masturbation is normal. And no matter what you hear, it definitely does not cause the long, grim list of ailments for which it often is blamed.

Probably the most important element in the situation is your attitude toward it. If you can regard masturbation as a part of the growing-up process, you will undoubtedly find that the youngster who is otherwise normally active masturbates at times.

The child for whom it becomes a problem is the one who feels guilty and fearful because he—or she—suspects that the parents would strongly disapprove. Parents often use threats that are very poor medicine indeed. A little boy should never be told, as all too many of them are, that if he masturbates he will lose his penis, or that it will be cut off. And a little girl should never be told that masturbation will prevent her from having a baby when she grows up. Tying the hands or other physical means of stopping the practice are also harsh and unsuccessful solutions. Making a child feel that he is "bad," "nasty," or "dirty" for masturbating is no help, either.

The best course, if you get a chance to talk about the subject, is to explain calmly that masturbation is neither wicked nor harmful. Explain, too, that most youngsters try it—some more than others—but that it is part of growth, an activity he will probably give up later.

For, as noted earlier, the only real harm from masturbation is the worry and anxiety that go with it. Even if little has been said about it, children often feel it's bad and that *something* will happen to them if they continue.

Children who masturbate a great deal, so that it interferes with their normal activities, are probably children who are unhappy and dissatisfied in many areas of their lives. They may spend much time alone, have trouble making friends, or show signs of not adjusting very well in other ways. This, of course, is not the result of masturbation. But masturbation, when it is extreme, is one of the signals that the child is in trouble and needs help. Professional advice is probably called for in these cases.

What is the parents' role during the five-to-eight period? The widening of your child's world will mean as much of an adjustment for you as for him. For now is the time when you must begin to let go of the reins a bit, to share him—and her—more generously. They are babies no longer. They must begin to work free of the family, to learn that affection, information, and guidance can come from sources other than the home.

Here are five points to keep in mind during this period:

1. Keep in touch with your child. Despite his strong urge to begin becoming an independent person in his own right, your child still thinks of home and family as the basis of his life and needs to feel that his place within them is secure. If you can keep in friendly touch with him, even though he doesn't need as much care as he used to, you will have a better idea of what he is about and what is going on within him.

He won't welcome poking and prying and close questioning. But try to listen. It is a child's impulse to show by word or deed much of what he is feeling and thinking—even as it is often the habit of parents to deafen themselves to the seemingly endless childish chatter. Allow the talk to register with you. Many child problems which parents "just can't understand" have, in fact, been spelled out for them by their youngsters many times over.

2. Try to do things with and for your child. What you do is less important than the fact that you're doing it. You need not be an entertainment committee for your child, but your age and good sense give you a better idea of what is possible at a given time or place. You can help your child widen his interests by making activities possible instead of forbidding them. This is particularly true if you are concerned about masturbation or sex play with other children and are trying to awaken the child to things outside himself.

Five to eight is a "doing" age for children. They like to see new places and pick up new facts. Every ride in the family car, every errand, every repair project around the home has the possibility of adventure to a child—and of fun for you.

This is a period when adults and children can have good times together. The young one has passed the unreliable baby stage. He can sit still for a greater span of time. He doesn't need to be fed or taken to the bathroom so often. He is alert and bright and thinks the world of you. Make the most of the opportunity. When adolescence rolls around, or even preadolescence, his own age group will surely be a more important source of fun than old-fogy adults.

This applies to work as well as to play. Encourage him to share in family chores and, where possible, in family responsibilities (feeding pets) and decisions (hamburgers or hot dogs, a movie or a ball game). Just be sure that the choices you put to him are ones he can make.

All of this takes patience. The child who wants to help Daddy with carpentering or Mommy in the kitchen cannot be kept interested very long if his effort is not a real one. This means that driving nails or mixing a cake must be learned and practiced, even at the cost of slowing down the adult's work.

It also means follow-through. One casual visit to a museum

will prove nothing if the child's newly awakened curiosity about stars or Indians or animals isn't helped along with talk around the table at home or a new book.

No matter how much he wants to be an individual, a child will not necessarily choose the best paths for himself. If he has nothing better than movies, comic books, and TV to stimulate his imagination, that is what he will feed on for the sense of adventure he needs.

3. Allow for mistakes. There will be many of them. A growing sense of self-confidence and a growing ability to choose almost certainly mean conflict or difficulty at some point. A child's choice may be a poor one, or it may be different from yours, but it becomes no choice at all if you second-guess or overrule him.

4. Be sympathetic. Your child is bound to overreach himself many times. He will insist on trying something he obviously can't do. He will find himself looking foolish. Or he will offend your sense of what is proper—or the neighbors'—with some clumsy remark or action.

In all these situations he will need adult help to bail himself out and to ease him through the embarrassment or guilt he feels. Avoid punishing words if you can. Very likely the child knows when he has behaved badly, and most children know it is not unreasonable that they face the consequences. What they don't understand is how they got into trouble and, often, why their behavior is undesirable. Kindly guidance, without sharp criticism, will help get them back on the track.

5. Be aware of yourself. At any point in your child's growth the most important help he will get will be the way his parents perform as adult human beings. As he sees that Mother enjoys her life as a woman and that Dad is glad to be a man, he, too, will feel comfortable and right about being what he is. Don't hesitate to tell him what you think and feel about important things of life. And encourage his response. You want to know his ideas, too.

The special tasks of creating a home and family are not particularly easy, but the spirit in which they are done will go far in setting a child's attitude toward the masculine or feminine role he or she will take on in later life.

A woman whose children's birthdays were approaching said to a friend that she was surprised and disappointed by the gifts they had asked for. The little girl, aged five, wanted a broom, dustpan, and carpet sweeper. The boy, seven, wanted a hammer, a saw, some nails, and some wood. Rather dull choices, the mother thought. "Perhaps," said the friend, "but rather a nice compliment, too. Your enjoyment of your home and the pleasure your husband gets from his workshop have been caught by the children. Their choice of gifts simply shows how much they want to be like you."

The opposite, of course, may also be true. Severe conflict and unhappiness will present a view of marriage that a child could hardly consider attractive or desirable.

Few homes offer a perfect surrounding for growing children. There is sure to be friction and disharmony at some points. This in itself is normal and not necessarily destructive. It is not the unevenness of the emotions around them that gets youngsters upset. It is the pretense and confusion that result from placing unreal values on the emotions that are expressed—for example, saying, "No, I'm not angry with you," through gritted teeth or saying, "That's just fine," half-heartedly or with a sigh. It is not necessary for you to be a perfect example for your children, but it is very important that you see as clearly as possible how you affect them. The more clearly you see yourself, and the more honestly you express yourself, the more surely you will be able to guide your children.

4 FACTS OF LIFE ILLUSTRATED

*Through the union of male
and female, the miracle of conception
takes place. Through pregnancy, the
incredible growth of a baby.
And through childbirth, the
renewal of life on earth.*

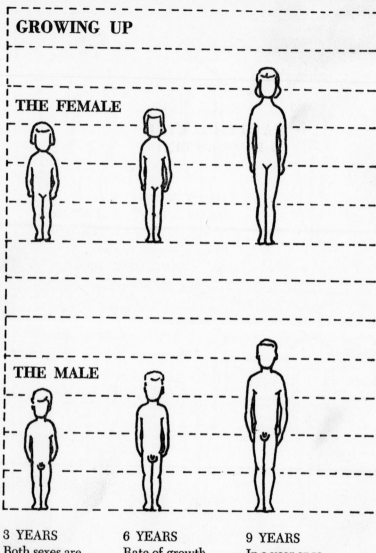

GROWING UP

THE FEMALE

THE MALE

3 YEARS
Both sexes are twice as big as at birth, but boy is slightly taller.

6 YEARS
Rate of growth is slower now, but boy holds lead in size over girl.

9 YEARS
In a year or so, girl will be bigger and more mature than boy

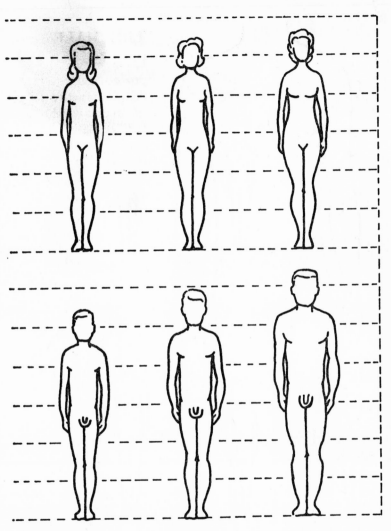

12 YEARS
Girl's hips widen,
breasts appear.
Boy's body is
still youthful.

15 YEARS
With spurt in
growth, boy now
passes girl in
size and weight

21 YEARS
Both are full grown.
(Patterns show
average;
individuals will
vary.)

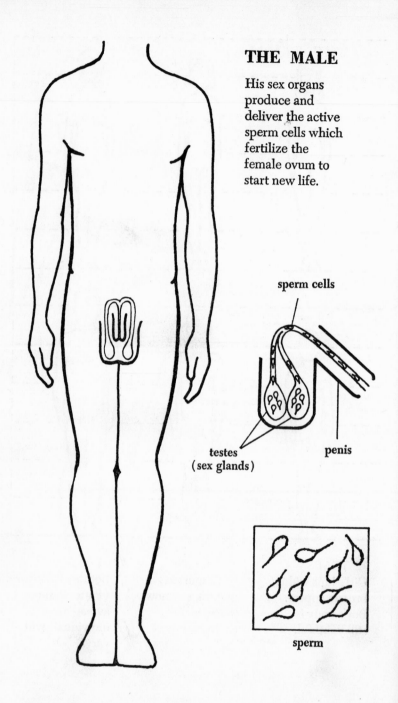

THE MALE

His sex organs produce and deliver the active sperm cells which fertilize the female ovum to start new life.

sperm cells

testes (sex glands)

penis

sperm

THE FEMALE

Her delicately
balanced sexual
system renews
itself each month
in preparation
for the role
of motherhood.

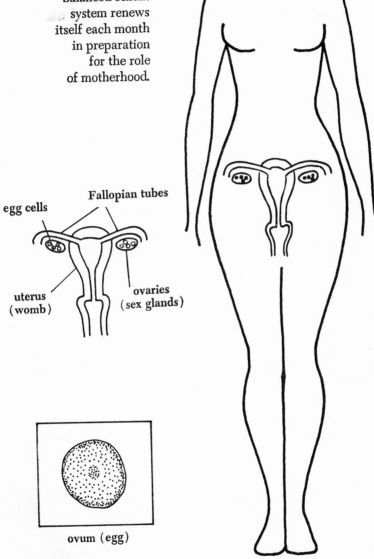

egg cells

Fallopian tubes

uterus
(womb)

ovaries
(sex glands)

ovum (egg)

THE BEGINNING OF LIFE

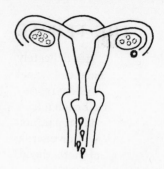

1 Father's sperm cells enter mother's vagina during intercourse. They move ...

4 Growth begins. Fertile cell subdivides many times. Each one has chromosomes which determine physical characteristics.

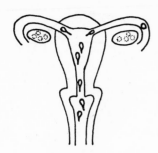

2 through uterus, propelled by whip-like tail, and into Fallopian tubes where . . .

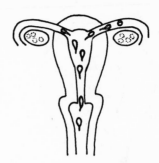

3 female ovum is being carried from ovary. Only one sperm can fertilize ovum.

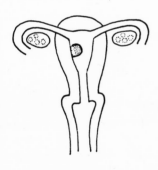

5 Cell moves into uterus, attaches itself to lining which stretches as baby develops.

6 In a month, dividing cells have become tiny human embryo fed via mother's blood.

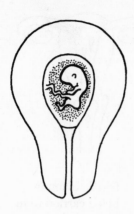

7 At two months,
embryo is only an
inch long but
form is human.
He floats . . .

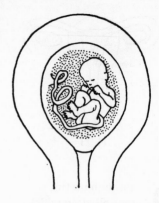

8 in "bag of waters,"
is nourished, by
fourth month
has become
four-ounce fetus.

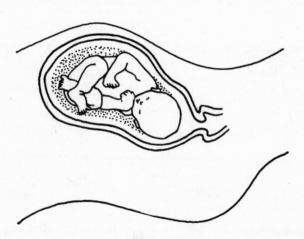

11 Birth begins sometime in ninth month.
Muscles of uterus contract to help push
baby out, waters ease . . .

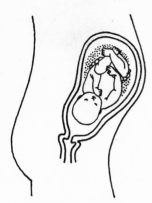

9 From six months on, baby's presence is very noticeable. Mother can feel movement . . .

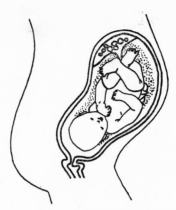

10 and he has shifted into head-down position in which he likely will be born.

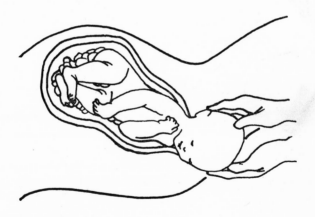

12 passage into world. With assist from doctor, baby becomes air-breathing member of human race.

5   PREADOLESCENCE

*Nearing the end of childhood,
boys and girls must be
prepared for the great and
vital changes which bring
the body to maturity.*

THE TIME OF GETTING READY

This is a time that tries the patience and understanding of even the best parents. For in preadolescence—roughly the period from nine to thirteen years of age—many children begin to act like hellions. They often are rude, sloppy, noisy, and disobedient. They tease. They are never on time. They don't bathe, pay attention, or sit still. They bicker among themselves, rebel against adults, and generally misbehave.

Why all this happens isn't definitely known. But if it is any comfort, this kind of unattractive behavior is apparently normal. This is not to say that the behavior can be ignored. It is to say that parents need every gift of tolerance, humor, and understanding they have.

What seems to be taking place in these youngsters is a period of getting ready for adolescence. And with it, the large discovery that there are ways of behaving in their own age group that are different from, and just as important as, those learned in the home. This may not be a surprising explanation, but it involves a number of difficult adjustments.

But there are advantages. All in all, despite his less lovable characteristics, the preadolescent is a realistic person whose blunt interest in facts makes him a good subject for certain aspects of sex education. Thus, while he may talk brashly and openly about sex, he is merely exercising his growing interest in all the facts of life. His own sexual development during this period is not very marked and he is not yet troubled by the urges of the adolescent.

"What is menstruation?"

At some time during this age span your daughter will want to know about menstruation. The word means "monthly flow" and it describes one part of the complex cycle by which the female body prepares itself every twenty-eight days (or so) for the conception and birth of a child.

Each month an egg cell, or ovum, is formed in one of a woman's two ovaries, the oval-shaped organs located at either side of her uterus, or womb, in the lower abdomen. When one of the egg cells leaves the ovary, it finds its way to the Fallopian tubes, one of which serves each ovary and leads to the uterus. This process is called ovulation. When the egg is fertilized by a male sperm cell in sexual intercourse, it travels down the tube and attaches itself to the wall of the uterus. Here it begins the great and complicated process of development into a baby. In getting ready for this process, the lining of the uterus has thickened with an extra supply of nourishing blood.

If fertilization does not take place, however, the uterus has no need for the lining (or endometrium) with its supply of blood, and it is cast off. This is the flow of blood from the vagina that happens during menstruation.

Each month the same process occurs. When it starts and how long it lasts may vary widely. In young girls the monthly periods may be irregular for quite some time. Eventually, however, it usually takes place approximately every twenty-eight days, and lasts from three to six days.

Be patient and be thorough in your explanation. What up to now has been a vague, far-off possibility is now becoming a reality to your daughter. Familiarity with the structure and functioning of her body will help give her a feeling of pride and satisfaction in being a girl.

"When does menstruation begin?"

Menstruation usually starts when a girl is between twelve and fourteen years of age. Each girl develops at her own pace, however, and it may begin earlier or later and still be quite normal for her.

In view of the uncertainty, it is wise to prepare your daughter for menstruation by age nine, so that when her first period comes it will be natural and expected even though the reality may be something of a shock.

Even before the first flow, most girls are interested in the practical details of what happens, and how. Mothers can help to prepare for a healthy acceptance of menstruation by the ease with which they explain it. There are, unfortunately, a number of fears and superstitions about menstruation even today. These have led women to regard it as a kind of illness and to describe it as "the curse" or "sick days." It is better to speak of "monthly periods" and to say that menstruation is simply a basic aspect of being a woman.

When the flow begins, a girl should be told how to wear sanitary pads, how to insure cleanliness, how much exercise to take, and what to do for the slight discomfort she may have. Today doctors agree that warm showers and baths are all right during menstruation, although cold water and chilling should be avoided. Mild exercise and a normal daily routine are helpful. Rest, aspirin, and a hot-water bottle usually relieve cramps. Severe pain, of course, should be treated by a doctor.

"When does menstruation end?"

Again, it depends on the individual. Generally, it ends between forty-five and fifty years of age. It may end abruptly or over a period of years. This is called the menopause, or "change of life," and marks the end of a woman's childbearing years. Menstruation also stops temporarily while a woman is pregnant.

"Why does menstruation begin before I want a baby?"

It's nature's way of making ready. It's a sign of growing up and of becoming a woman instead of a little girl, but it usually takes some time for the system to get itself in order. It may be some months before a girl's periods assume a regular pattern for her. And the beginning of menstruation does not always mean that a girl is immediately fertile—that her ova are ready to be impregnated and develop into babies. Mainly, though, it's simply a stage of growth which happens and thus may occur before a person is ready to make use of it.

"Does ovulation or menstruation hurt?"

Usually menstruation does not cause pain. Some girls have menstrual cramps, though—often as the result of tenseness or worry. If your daughter's periods are painful, check with your doctor.

"I'm afraid of menstruation. Why is it necessary?"

Some girls are worried or depressed by menstruation. Some are far from happy about the change that has taken place within them, although they are not likely to be entirely clear about what makes them unhappy and why, and may not want to discuss it with anyone. And although it would seem obvious, they may not even relate their melancholy to menstruation. They are quietly tense, sometimes flare up irritably, often begin to do poorly in school. They may lose their appetite or overeat. They may sleep restlessly at night.

More information probably is not the answer to this situation. It is not what the girl knows but what she is feeling that needs attention. Menstruation is a symbol of advancement toward maturity—a state that a girl may desire and dread at the same time. She should be helped to feel that menstruation is a sign of growing up—a sign of womanhood. If a woman did not menstruate, she could not bear children.

Satisfy yourself first that troublesome trifles have been met. Sometimes a girl may feel odd and set apart by being the first of her friends to menstruate; reassurance and the passage of time will erase this. Sometimes the sanitary pads and belt are uncomfortable and a nuisance; mothers can help by seeing to a proper fitting.

But beyond this there may be discomfort over the fact of growth itself. However much parents wish it, there is no simple formula for adjusting this difficulty. As has been noted, we more or less pile up the unlearned lessons of the past and carry them with us into maturity. Turning points in life, like menstruation, are likely to bring our weaknesses and unreadiness to the surface where our fears of them are reflected in everyday behavior.

It is not easy to make up for lost "growing time," yet it can be done with sympathy, understanding, and patience. If it seems to be more than you can cope with alone, however, do not hesitate to get professional assistance.

"What's the matter with her?"

Your boy may wonder why his sister doesn't join wholeheartedly at play at certain times of the month. This is a good time to tell him that she is having a menstrual period. Then explain in somewhat more detail.

Factually, boys should know as much about menstruation as girls do, although the knowledge is not necessary at so early an age. In times past it was considered an indelicate business that men ignored as being of no concern to them. Yet to gain an honest, realistic picture of human sexuality it is important that boys understand and appreciate the menstrual cycle. Girls should know about the male sexual system, too.

"Why do boys have 'wet dreams'?"

This is where it is preferable for the father to step in. There is no reason why either parent cannot explain sex to children of either sex. Yet there are stages of development where it seems more convincing for the child to talk to an adult of the same sex, who has gone through the same experience.

The situation is most natural, of course, if Dad has been his boy's friend all along. If he has been content to let Mother take care of these "chores" up to now, he is going to find sex a sensitive and difficult subject upon which to start basing a relationship. There had best be some of the give-and-take which makes people real personalities to each other before Dad tries to start cold on the facts of life.

Preadolescent boys, of course, do not have to be prepared for a sexual change as dramatic as menstruation. But they should be told of the changes that will affect them between the ages of thirteen and fifteen. They should know that "wet dreams" are seminal emissions that occur during the night. These nocturnal emissions are normal, as are the sex dreams that often go with them. They should know where the semen is produced, how it is stored, and why the discharges occur. They should know that the production of semen is one of the signs of truly growing up and becoming a man. A scientific lecture isn't necessary, but youngsters as well as their parents generally feel more comfortable discussing sexual matters when they are familiar with the proper terms.

The "wet dream"—or emission of semen during sleep—is caused by an accumulation of excess semen, which gathers in the tubes leading from the testes when a person has had no occasion to release it in intercourse or otherwise. It might even be compared to a reservoir into which water continually flows and from which no water is taken. When the reservoir becomes full, the excess water will overflow its banks.

Three organs prepare the semen. The testes provide the spermatozoa. The seminal vesicles and the prostate, a gland the size of a chestnut that lies at the base of the bladder, produce a secretion that mixes with the sperm cells and carries them out. It may help to add that the male sex cells are able, unlike the female ova, to propel themselves by way of a whiplike tail. This ability to move enables a sperm cell—one of the millions discharged in sexual intercourse—to reach the Fallopian tube and join with a female ovum to make it fertile.

The seminal fluid, with its numberless spermatozoa, flows through tubes called the vas deferens and into the penis, from which it is discharged.

Father may not be any more at ease than Mother in telling these facts to their sons, but, like most parents, he will find that after taking the plunge the problem is to know when and where to stop. A casual and friendly conversation while doing a job or taking a walk together should break down the reserve that father or son may feel.

"What else should I know about intercourse?"

You will probably have told your child something about intercourse by this time, but he'll want to know more details. You can explain that intercourse is the physical act of mating when two people care for each other and want to be close. The male sperm comes from the father's penis and joins the female egg cell inside the mother's body.

"How is intercourse carried out?"

At this age, a child will probably not be satisfied with a single, simple statement. Don't hold back; he can handle it. Tell him that during intercourse, the father's penis increases in length, becomes stiff, and stands out from the body. This is an erection. It enables the father to insert the penis into the mother's vagina, where the cells are released in what is called seminal fluid.

"Does a baby start every time you mate?"

No. Unless a male cell finds and penetrates a female ovum a baby will not be started. This does not always happen in intercourse. You might go on to explain that just one ovum is formed each month, and there are just a few days when it is possible for the male cell to fertilize it.

"What is the male sperm like?"

It is shaped like a tiny tadpole. It has a round head and a long, tapering tail that whips back and forth to propel it through the uterus and Fallopian tube. About five hundred of them would measure an inch. For a more detailed explanation of how sperm cells are produced, stored and discharged, see the question on seminal emissions on page 65.

"What is the female egg cell like?"

If your child wonders about the male sperm cell, he'll certainly want to know about the female egg cell. It is round and about the size of a pinpoint—about 125 times the size of the sperm cell. It has no power to move itself. For more information about the female egg, see the question on menstruation on page 60.

"How does the cell turn into a baby?"

Once a male sperm cell has entered an ovum it is fertilized and begins an active process known as cell division. The single cell becomes two, then four, and so on and some cells become fingers and toes, legs and arms, nerves and muscles, etc. By the time a baby is ready to be born his body contains billions of cells. The development of the fertilized ovum into a baby about to be born is a thrilling thing, and the preadolescent child should understand all of these facts.

"Why does a baby look like its parents?"

Both the male and female cells have a nucleus—a core, or central point—which contains chromosomes. Chromosomes are made up of many thousands of tiny parts called genes. The genes from the cells of the parents are responsible for such inherited characteristics as the color of a person's eyes or hair or skin, the shape of his features, the general build of his body. Because the genes mingle, a child rarely looks exactly like either parent, but he may have "his mother's eyes" or "his father's nose." Pick up a mirror and let him see which of his features resemble yours, which are like your mate's, and which are uniquely his.

"What decides the baby's sex?"

This is a natural follow-up to the previous question. The sex is determined by chromosomes, too. It is the male cell which decides, but it is impossible to control or predict whether a child will be boy or girl.

"What causes twins?"

Cell division takes place within the covering or shell of the original cell. However, if the cell should split into two separate cells during the first division, two babies will develop. These are called identical twins and will look and act almost exactly like each other throughout life.

Explain that fraternal twins, which don't necessarily look like each other and may even be boy and girl, are the result of two separate egg cells being fertilized, each by a different male cell.

"What causes birthmarks?"

Youngsters seem to be particularly interested in anyone who is not perfectly normal physically, and this includes people with birthmarks. These are skin blemishes which may be caused by a concentration of blood or of skin coloring at one spot. They are not and cannot be caused by a fright or shock to the mother during pregnancy.

"How do you know you're going to have a baby?"

The mother realizes it first when she misses a menstrual period. She may also miss a period occasionally for other reasons, but it is one of the definite signs of pregnancy. Later she may also feel nausea, or "morning sickness," upon awakening. (You might reassure your daughter that "morning sickness" is really a trivial thing—not serious, not important.) Usually she has a checkup with a doctor, who can make any one of several tests to tell for sure.

If she is pregnant, she can figure that the baby will arrive about 280 days, or nine months, from the time of her last menstrual period.

"How is the baby born?"

When the time comes, the mother gets signals from her abdominal muscles. These flex rhythmically and steadily to push the baby out into the world through the vagina. This passage expands to permit the baby's birth. Usually, baby comes head first, but he may come feet first or seat first. Doctors are prepared to handle the situation in any case. Childbirth is often painful—your child should know this—but the body is made to manage the process naturally and successfully.

"Do unmarried people ever have babies?"

Yes. A grown-up man and woman can have a baby whether they are married or not if their bodies are physically ready. However, in our society it is considered both morally and legally wrong to have intercourse—with the possibility of pregnancy—before you are married. Thus the unmarried couple may have a difficult time, and their baby, too. For they will find it hard to give him the steady care and love that a home and married life permit. Usually parents are married first because this means they have chosen to live their lives together, to have a home and to bring up their children together.

FOR THE PARENT

Do preadolescents develop a sudden, strong interest in sex? Parents sometimes have reason to think so. A thirteen-year-old who has recently been happily occupied in schoolwork, his friends, his chemistry set, and his Scout troop may suddenly show an alarming appetite for lurid and trashy magazines. He may pore over adult books he has heard are sexy, be curious about movies advertised as for "adults only," and read intently the stories of criminal sex behavior in the newspapers.

These interests are surprising to parents mostly because they are such a change from the child's apparent recent unconcern with sex. But in this the child is by no means abnormal. He is probably trying to satisfy his curiosity about a new aspect of life.

The younger child's lack of interest in sex is actually not quite what it seems. Children never really lose interest in sex, although from time to time it fades into the background while they deal with more pressing problems, such as learning to make friends, adjusting to school, or finding their way in the world outside the home. Sooner or later, however, they are bound to have their interest reawakened and will bring it out into the open.

How do I deal with it? Be sure of yourself and of the situation before you plunge in. Consider your child as a whole person. His sexual curiosity can't override everything else in life, and if he seems to be keeping up with his friends and his other activities there is not much to be concerned about. As he reads or talks about his discoveries you will find chances to set him straight and elaborate on what he wants to know.

His interest in sex may not seem very wholesome. But preadolescents don't like generalizations about the beauty and poetry

of life. Their steel-trap minds are much more likely to fasten on
the gory detail, or on the sensational and unusual. This is not
uncommon or unhealthy. They know that rape and adultery occur,
that children are born out of wedlock. Of course, how much is
clearly understood and how much only felt as "something wrong"
depends on the child. In any event, you can take advantage of
this curiosity by giving the child the information he needs as spe-
cifically as possible. Don't be afraid to mention the violent and
tragic side of life. You can't keep these facts from the youngster
forever, and his reading or hearing about them will help him in
some degree to work off, in imagination, the aggression and rebellion he feels in himself. Keep your explanation of such situations
matter-of-fact, however, and use the opportunity to give a balanced view, so that he does not get the idea that these troubles
are the rule rather than the exception.

If sexual curiosity continues and seems too intense or troubling,
think back and see whether there has been a recent event in the
youngster's life which may be troubling him. Very often, even at
this age, a new baby in the family will stir up old worries in the
child about his place in his parents' affections, or about the meaning of sex relations. A drastic shift in the family routine, the death
or absence of a parent, a move to a strange town, a new school,
or money troubles in the family may be making life difficult for
him. Upset and unsure of himself, he may be unable to handle
what ordinarily would be a normal increase in sexual interest.
He will probably welcome any effort by you to help him with
the problems that are nagging him and to steer him into other
channels of activity.

Whenever you can, look behind puzzling behavior for possible
causes, and if you can't find them, don't hesitate to get professional advice.

What questions do preadolescents ask? Generally they ask the
same questions they've asked you before. The terms are more

grown up. Naturally they have a better idea of life's processes. But they still aren't sure. Sometimes they'll sound as though they'd never been told anything. Even so, they are ready for more exact knowledge. They should know more exactly about sexual intercourse and reproduction. They can be told more facts about their own bodily functions as future fathers and mothers. At this age, too, children begin to understand the love aspects of the sexual relationship. Remember to bring this up when you discuss sex with them.

The preadolescents' great ability to catch on and remember makes this an especially good time to give the exact words and terms of sex, too. They will take what you tell them simply as additions to their store of facts, and you will save yourself the trouble of re-educating them later on, in adolescence.

What if my child never asks questions? Even when parents are ready and willing to talk frankly, some children still find it hard to think and talk about sex. They seem, for reasons that aren't always clear, to fear their own curiosity, and, therefore, to smother it. Others, of course, react the same way because they may have found from past experience that grownups are embarrassed by talk of sex and try to avoid it. Such children usually consult their friends and keep quiet at home.

Look at your own attitude toward sex first, and at how much you have already talked with your child about it and in what way. If your performance has been incomplete, unclear, or dull, admit it. This will at least give you a basic point to start from and a chance to get on a more realistic footing with your child.

If the child's silence is a new and puzzling turn in your relationship up to now, you may have to make openings in order to give him the information he needs to know, or to bring out the fears that have bottled him up.

Behavior, as well as questions, may indicate whether a child has something stewing inside him. Don't wait him out. A marriage, a pregnancy, a miscarriage, or a birth, in the family or in the neighborhood, are all quite natural events which you can bring up casually as starting points for a talk. If the child opens up, you can carry the discussion as far as seems helpful. If the child reacts uneasily, drop the subject until another time. There are plenty of moments when parents can comment on sex, just as they would on anything else that interests a child. And when the child discovers that his parents can talk freely, he becomes less fearful of his own curiosity and can air his thoughts.

Won't children discuss what they know with their friends? Quite likely they will. Talk about sex is quite as possible as any other kind of talk among youngsters. It does no harm so long as children don't get in the habit of looking only to their friends for information, but feel free to turn to their parents, too. Holding back information because it might be blurted around the neighborhood is poor policy. One way or another, you may be sure that preadolescents will learn about sex. And the child whose instruction has not been thorough is defenseless against unpleasant and perhaps frightening misinformation.

As a social matter, however, it is quite all right for parents to urge their children not to parade their knowledge around in public. Not because there is anything wrong with the knowledge as such, but because every parent prefers to handle the matter his own way with his own children. Frankness within the family is one thing; when it concerns sex, a little frankness goes a long way in most social groups. This is merely a matter of custom that children should soon understand and observe.

What about books that explain sex? Books are fine for adding to the facts of sex you have told your preadolescent, but they should not be his first or only guide. Books may give the story of sex more accurately and completely than you can. Many of them are also quite helpful in giving a natural, happy view of the emotional side of sex.

A book, however, can't always answer what happens to be on a child's mind in a particular way at a particular time. And it is, of course, silent and impersonal. It can never supply the affection that passes between parent and child in a relaxed and friendly conversation.

If you are a little shaky on the facts yourself, get a book or two, by all means. And if it seems like a good way to get into the subject, read the book aloud with your child.

Other facts about preadolescents. When you look at your preadolescent ten-, eleven- or twelve-year-old, you can easily see that he is no longer a child, quite. And, at the same time, he is too childish—physically, mentally, and emotionally—to think and act like a teen-ager. Whether boy or girl, many preadolescents have slim, trim, Peter Pan shapes. In any event, the ten- to twelve-year-old's body is more muscular, better co-ordinated and faster growing than that of the little five- to nine-year-old. But it is still more juvenile than that of the maturing adolescent. The preadolescent has about as much physical vigor as he will ever have again. He is remarkably free of illness—possibly because he is never in one place long enough for a germ to catch him! Both boys and girls are extremely restless. Their hands are constantly in motion—picking, pulling, scratching, twisting. Much of this action is aimless, but much of it is used in learning how to play baseball or tennis, in mastering the piano, in painting or in handicrafts. Often they swing from periods of great activity to spells of daydreaming. What do they dream of? Returning slowly from far away, they will tell you "nothing."

Mentally, they are great fact-finders and are grown-up enough to fit what they discover into their youthful world. They do not ask the endless, unconnected "why" questions of the little tyke. They begin to grasp the physical facts of why clocks run and jet planes fly and that what goes up must come down. Often they read enormously, some of them quite as well as the average adult.

Why do children join groups or gangs? This is a period when boys and girls begin to join in groups or gangs of children of their own sex. At this stage boys and girls are indifferent to, or even quite hostile toward, each other, and their relations are full of teasing and bickering. Almost entirely, boys prefer to play with boys and girls with girls—hence, the group associations which both tend to form.

Only when the group's boundless energy has no useful outlet is trouble likely to arise. For by its nature, a group is aggressive and puts a high value on the courage, strength, and loyalty of its members. Although this often results in some rebellion against adult rules, the group can be very important in what it does for a boy's feeling about being male. In showing off their maleness, of course, boys frequently place more stock in the attitudes and opinions of their friends than in those of the parents, especially the mother, whose influence may be regarded as "sissy." Secrets— codes, passwords, and similar excitement—also serve to build up preadolescent independence and show adults that they don't know everything.

Use good judgment, however. You needn't surrender completely to the group. The standards of a child's friends must be taken into account, but not necessarily approved 100 per cent. Children at this age need help from parents to stand up for what's right even when it runs against group opinions. They should be encouraged to weigh the customs and prejudices of those around them before accepting them. It is not easy to do, but it is basic to a real feeling of independence, and young people appreciate parents who show themselves ready to act on their own views of right and wrong.

What if my child uses "bad" language? First of all, expect it. Either innocently or to create a small sensation, children will try out swear words or crude sexual terms at home. Nothing will be gained by acting shocked or horrified, or by punishing the child. Remember that the first swearing a child hears quite often comes from his parents.

Even so, you don't have to ignore the issue or pretend that you enjoy "bad" language around the home. Let the child know that the words are no surprise, that you know what they mean. If he doesn't, incidentally, it may be necessary to explain them briefly, unpleasant as that may be, just to keep him from thinking there is something mysterious and special about them.

Having done that, however, you can make it plain, without heat, that such talk is a form of bad manners, like nose-picking or undressing in public, and that people just don't like it. It offends against the customs by which most people live.

It's entirely possible that a preadolescent will use the words or tell the "dirty" jokes he hears simply to annoy. If general suggestions to stop the talk don't work, it may be—again—a symptom of other trouble. It may be wise to look further to see what is making him behave this way.

Generally, except among themselves where profanity may be a badge of belonging to a group, children do not concern themselves very much with "bad" language once they have found out what it is.

How can I be a better parent? Parents are often upset to find their preadolescent children difficult to live with. They wonder and worry about what they are "doing wrong." It is hard to persuade them that a child's unpleasing behavior can be a perfectly normal follow-up to the stable years that went before. Their own uncertainty is increased by the preadolescent's absolute certainty that he is greatly misunderstood and badly treated.

If these are your feelings, don't surrender to them. Whatever his manner, the preadolescent, like every child at every age, needs your guidance and support. Keep in mind that he is struggling to live up to two standards of behavior—yours and his age-group's—which at many points are bound to clash. Yours may have more sense and more experience behind them, but they are not necessarily the only ones from which he can learn. He rates a chance to apply what he has learned from you, to vary it, and even to choose—as he will have to do as an adult—other courses for himself. Here are some of the ways parents meet common situations:

"Wherever did you hear that?" Most conflict arises when mothers or fathers feel that a youngster's every new opinion is a challenge to their own wisdom and must be fitted into their pattern or stamped out. Learn to give a little. Don't hold on to your authority at the expense of the child's effort to widen his horizon.

"All right, if you have to learn the hard way." Parents hope, naturally enough, that their youngsters will learn without pain the hard lessons of growing up. Unfortunately, it doesn't seem possible. The child who is working his way toward adult maturity is going to trip over his own feet and step on yours doing it. There's no other way to discover the true meaning of independence. When you try to mastermind the process, or control it, or protect against it, the child is boxed in by your judgment and your experience. This may make him too dependent, a youngster without much will or spunk of his own. Every child is struggling to be himself at this age. Help him along.

"The idea! Talking to your parents that way!" Perhaps the single most important thing that can be said is: don't get booby-trapped by your child's surface behavior. Don't take it at face value; it is not a fair or complete expression of him as a person. And avoid reacting to it on his level.

This is not easy advice to follow. You may ask yourself what happened to the smiling, loving, easy-going youngster of a year or two ago. But keep telling yourself that the good stuff is there. For beneath the foolishness and stubbornness and unreasonableness, it is. Basic quality doesn't disappear overnight and forever. With encouragement your child will come out of this period with a new ability to meet new hurdles.

"I think you're absolutely right." Find ways, if you can, to show your faith and confidence in him. For while he feels he must dispute your wisdom and favor his own, he just isn't that sure of himself. Admit his good judgments and back them—and even some that don't appeal to you if they obviously are important and not harmful to him. Accept his friends. Remember that loyalty to his pals is important to him. Don't let him feel that you have rejected him, or withdrawn your interest and affection, because of his strange behavior. As with children of any age, look for opportunities to involve him in family activities. The preadolescent generally enjoys taking part in jobs he regards as grown-up. Boys like to show off their growing strength by toting bulky packages. Girls enjoy planning and cooking an entire meal, rather than just setting the table.

"I wonder—am I doing the right thing?" Have faith and confidence in yourself, too. For let it be said here and now that there's no magic to come to your rescue. Your understanding will not suddenly make your preadolescent a lovely, obedient child. He will be strengthened by your support—as you will see in his handling of adolescence—but he will not be bribed by it.

Your child's need to grow up and to be different from you by being himself cannot be stopped. Your hope must be that he will continue to want your affection and respect your opinions.

"Well, let's see if we can't compromise." This ties to the point of not responding to preadolescent behavior on its own level. A helpful attitude from you, after all, is a mature attitude—

the attitude of the adult your youngster is trying to become. Adults who show childish irritation or closed-mindedness give the preadolescent an out-of-focus picture of maturity, and set up a vicious circle of conflict and rebelliousness between themselves and their children.

This does not mean, of course, that you must take rude behavior with a glad smile. That's unrealistic, too. You have rights and privileges as a person that others—preadolescent or not—should honor. You needn't be a doormat. On the other hand, you needn't take every sharp preadolescent remark as a personal insult.

Love grows. What is often lost sight of in the wrangles and the outbursts of preadolescence is that much of this struggle is necessary for the development of sound and healthy emotions. At this age, children still have a long way to go in settling their own basic feelings of maleness and femaleness, and in developing a sense of their own identity they need to build relationships with other males and females. Boys and girls must still look to their parents for this practice and experience. In infancy they learn to take affection. In the early years of childhood they learned to give it. In preadolescence their giving, ideally, is expanded. They find room in their affections for animal pets, for special friends and playmates, and for adult outsiders as well as relatives. It will not always seem so to you. Yet the capacity is there. And it grows.

Affection and regard for another person, of course, are the basis of later sexual relations. During preadolescence, see that your child is fully informed in sexual matters, so that his emotional relations with the opposite sex, which will soon begin to blossom, are honest and as free of fear and anxiety as possible.

6 TEEN-AGERS

They must seek the rich range of emotion that will give meaning and expression to the new, adult sensations of their bodies.

THE EDGE OF MATURITY

It is in the teen-age years of adolescence that the parents' role in sex education is perhaps most vital. This is a period of many changes extending over a number of years, which are often baffling and sometimes seemingly more childish than adult. But by the time young people graduate from high school, they are in most respects grown up.

As they pass through the years from fourteen to nineteen, your children gradually reach physical maturity. Except for some pounds and inches they may still add in the next year or so, they are full grown. The gangly teen-age boy fills out; his hands and feet no longer seem impossibly large. His cracking, reedy voice develops a manly tone. He will begin to shave. His sexual organs mature.

Even more complex changes take place in the girl. Her form will slowly lose its sexless, little-girl slenderness. Her hips will widen to enable her to carry and bear a baby. Her breasts will develop. Her menstrual cycle will settle into what for her will be a regular pattern.

Ready or not, by the time they reach nineteen, the boy is considered a man and the girl a woman. Henceforth, they are young grown-ups, able to live their own lives. It is to this point that all the chapters of this book are aimed. It is a point easy to lose sight of in the thousands of days and numberless small events that finally lead up to it. Few parents are wise or bold enough to predict the final outcome of one decision or another made for their small children along the way. Yet all of us know that the sum total of our decisions has a definite effect on the kind of personality and kind of citizen we eventually give to the world.

Adolescence, the final stage of growth through which our children pass, is also the longest. This is probably fortunate, for it is also in many ways the most difficult and, therefore, one of our great opportunities as parents to guide a youngster helpfully and effectively.

"Should teen-agers go steady?"

There is no "right" answer to this question. It depends on the individuals involved and on the degree of maturity they have shown in their relationships with other boys and girls so far. It also depends on the community in which they live and on family background. What is proper in one town may be considered scandalous in another. What one custom or tradition encourages, another may discourage.

Even so, there are some general considerations that young people—and their parents—might take into account before deciding one way or the other.

Most adolescent boy-girl relationships are a normal development of interest in the other sex and are not too intense or lasting. Going to the movies, having a "Coke date," and dancing, walking, or playing games together are the ways young people get to know each other as people and as members of the opposite sex. Showing consideration and affection for each other is also part of the experience. Such attachments are real as long as they last, and can be looked at as practice for the more permanent love relationships that come later.

Occasionally, of course, boys and girls will become serious about each other, and they'll go steady or worry about whether they should. This is a time for tolerance, patience, and understanding by all concerned. If the youngsters' background of human relations and sexual understanding is good, a deep emotional experience in these years—permanent or not—may have real value. Parents often are troubled about "going steady," and there are disadvantages to it. But it should be remembered that an experience which has depth of feeling gives another dimension to a youthful personality—and that if real depth is lacking the relationship will soon wear itself out, anyway.

On the other hand, it often is not very wise for youngsters to become too deeply involved. The teens are a time to get a variety of experience and to know a number of different boys and girls. Only by running into and responding to different temperaments, interests, and points of view can a young person begin to select those he values most. It is a rare youngster whose experience and judgment are broad enough in adolescence to pick a compatible lifetime partner (or who is settled enough economically to support one).

Adolescents may also be too close to the people with whom they have grown up to seek anything but a copy of what they know, whether good or bad. A boy sees in his girl something that reminds him of his mother. A girl is attracted to a fellow because he has her dad's sense of humor. If recognized for what they are, these values are quite all right. But they are not necessarily a basis for a complete and lasting relationship.

Parents should not be in a hurry to point out errors in their young people's judgment. No one will turn a deaf ear so quickly as the youngster whose loved one is criticized. You can, however, help him—or her—to see and think about his "affair" in relation to other interests and goals.

Above all, try to avoid teasing and joking about your children's boy and girl friends. Very often these are quite tender situations in which the youngster is fairly unsure of himself. To be laughed at and made to seem foolish may turn a son or daughter away from his parents and also make it difficult for him in starting future relationships.

"Should teen-agers neck or pet?"

Some physical expression of affection between boys and girls is normal and probably necessary. Hand-holding, kissing, and simple caressing is usual behavior between youngsters who enjoy each other, and nothing to get alarmed about.

Does the activity stop at that, though? Every parent worries. How do you stop it at that? Every teen-ager wonders. There is no doubt but that it is a fairly short step from the childish games and dancing by which youngsters first make contact with each other to the more adult sexual exploration we call necking or petting.

As a general rule, adolescents are guided by the standards of their families and the customs of their community. At the same time, eighteen- or nineteen-year-olds don't always know what to expect of themselves or each other in a sexual situation, or how to keep it from getting out of control. Boys discover that touching a girl's breasts or genitals prompts a warm response. And this, in turn, heightens his own male sexual urge, producing an erection and a need for release through an ejaculation, or expulsion of semen. Stimulation of the girl may arouse in her a mounting desire which is totally satisfied only by intercourse. (In many adolescent girls a conscious desire for sexual intercourse takes time to develop. In others, just as normal, it may be as specific as in the male.)

There is nothing unusual about these feelings, as any adult knows. They are the feelings which man and wife arouse in each other by the embraces or wooing that begin adult intercourse.

The older teen-ager, however, is faced with two unhappy choices. Either he must bring his urges to a highly unsatisfactory halt, or he must continue on to intercourse which carries risks and a burden of guilt. While there may be a temptation to be swept away by the passions of the hour, most young people know, in cooler moments, that they are not really ready for intercourse.

Most are seeking a balance between their long-range goals and their immediate desires. They are trying to become mature adults.

In this, parents can help, first, by respecting their children's efforts and avoiding the suspicions, the too-close questioning, and the overly harsh restrictions that may make a child feel he's not trusted. By looking honestly at their own beliefs and sharing them with their children, parents can also do much to strengthen a teenager's ability to make sound ethical decisions for himself. It will help your teen-ager to know that you had these same feelings and struggles when you were his age.

"What about premarital intercourse?"

Most parents tell their children that intercourse is best reserved for marriage. Young people usually understand the situation and try to hold down their desires until the approved time.

There are solid reasons for this. We are all members of a society. As such, we must try to work within the framework of behavior the society has chosen for itself. We must at least try to be constructive, to center our lives around basic expectations and convictions. Many find the answers to such questions as the rightness or wrongness of premarital intercourse in religion, while others struggle along searching for the answers on their own. But whatever the course, everyone must find something—a code or "philosophy of life"—to live by.

In our society there is a basic moral objection to intercourse out of wedlock. There is also the fact that few young people can afford the risk of having a baby before they can give it a stable and secure home.

All of these factors may fall by the wayside when a boy and a girl in their late teens find themselves with the desire and the opportunity to have sex relations. Yet a secret, out-of-bounds affair is a strain on both partners—mostly, as it turns out, because they are not really partners. They are sharing an adventure which carries no responsibility with it and can be broken off at any time by either one—perhaps even for reasons that have nothing to do with the relationship. It is an unsteady situation at best, and one which can bring heartbreak and bitterness to one or both.

It is natural to want to be wanted and to try to please the one from whom affection comes. But teen-agers rarely have had enough experience with a variety of people to know definitely what is genuine regard and what is a passing infatuation. Until they do, intercourse is best left alone. For sexual relations, as has been said elsewhere in this book, are the expression of our deepest feelings for a person who has worth and meaning for us. These are not feelings to be treated lightly.

Item: However much more relaxed our standards may be these days, loss of virginity through premarital intercourse may be deeply regretted later on.

Item: So far, we have no proof that premarital intercourse makes either person a better sexual partner in marriage.

"What is birth control?"

What parents tell their children about birth control will depend, of course, on their own beliefs as to the right and wrong of it. If they have religious or personal reasons for thinking it to be wrong, they should say so when the question arises, explaining clearly what their judgment is based upon.

Likewise, parents who believe that birth control—or planned parenthood, as it is often called—has meant a step forward in human welfare will want to explain to their growing sons and daughters why they believe this is so.

But children should be told the basic facts when they ask. Birth control is the act of regulating conception. It means choosing the time you have a baby. There are several safe and effective ways to do this. These can be prescribed by your doctor when you are going to be married. It is vital to tell teen-agers who ask for more specific information that no one method of birth control is the answer for everyone and this should be individually prescribed by a doctor.

Older children are likely to have heard of contraception—ways to prevent the male sperm from fertilizing the female ovum—and will be curious about it. This may be another chance to talk over the feelings and emotions that are so vital a part of the sex life of human beings. When a man and woman are deeply in love, having sex relations gives them a special feeling of closeness and harmony and of joy in each other. Yet it may not always be a wise thing for them to have a child. There may be health, financial, or other reasons for preventing conception or controlling the length of time between pregnancies.

"Is masturbation harmful in adolescence?"

No. A certain amount of it—by both boys and girls—is usual. It serves as a release for sexual tensions the youngster feels strongly and frequently at this time. As in the earlier years, however, excessive masturbation is nearly always an indication of inner conflict and disturbance and calls for professional guidance.

"What happens in pregnancy?"

This is the period of forty weeks in which a fertilized ovum about the size of a dot at the end of a sentence develops into a baby ready to begin life. The ovum travels down its Fallopian tube and enters the uterus. There it attaches itself to the uterine wall—the special lining which is thrown off in menstruation if not needed—and begins a process of subdivision.

The first outward sign of pregnancy is the stopping of menstruation. Later there will be others; the enlargement of breasts and nipples, for example. And beyond the fourth month, the abdomen is noticeably larger.

Meanwhile, the baby is developing rapidly. At the end of the first month it is a quarter inch in size; by the end of the second it is three quarters of an inch. At this stage it is called an embryo. At four months, it is five inches long, has a definitely human form, and is called a fetus. The features of the face have appeared and so have the external genitals. The fingers and toes are separate.

In the fifth month, the mother will begin to feel life inside her—stirrings and tappings and, later on, an occasional very noticeable kick.

Throughout pregnancy, the baby is cushioned against injury by the "bag of waters," a sac of fluid which surrounds him and in which he floats. Across one end of the sac is an organ known as the placenta, which is attached to the wall of the uterus. Through this organ, and by way of the umbilical cord, the baby receives nourishment and oxygen from the mother and gets rid of his waste products. At birth its usefulness comes to an end. It is cut and tied, and where it was attached to the body becomes the navel.

"How is a baby born?"

Some 280 days from the start of the mother's last menstrual period, birth begins. Just which day it will be, and whether mother or baby starts the process, is not known. But mother knows the time has come when she feels the muscles of her uterus begin to tense and relax, slowly but steadily. This is the beginning of labor, the process by which the baby is pushed into the world.

There is no way to tell how long it will last. It depends upon the individual. First babies usually take longer than later ones.

The first stage may last from nine to fourteen hours. Contractions of the uterine muscles begin, continuing with shorter and shorter intervals between them. The cervix, the opening at the bottom end of the uterus which leads into the vagina, is spreading wide to permit passage of the child.

In the second stage of labor (one to two hours), the child emerges into the world. The bag of water bursts and the baby gradually pushes through the vagina to the outside. Usually he comes head first.

The final stage of labor (just a few minutes) is elimination of the placenta and the sac that contained the baby. This happens within a half-hour after the baby has been born. The placenta and sac are called, quite logically, the "afterbirth."

The umbilical cord is cut and tied by the doctor. The baby cries, thus starting his lungs working on the lifelong task of breathing air. Medicine is dropped into his eyes to kill any possible infection. And the process is complete.

"What is a miscarriage?"

A miscarriage is the birth of a baby who has not developed enough to be able to live. It may be the result of a defective ovum that cannot develop into a normal baby, or of some weakness or illness that affects the mother. Many women have miscarriages and then go on to have any number of normal pregnancies.

"What is a Caesarean birth?"

This is a surgical operation to deliver a baby which, in a doctor's judgment, cannot or should not be born in the usual way. It is performed by cutting through the abdomen and into the uterus and removing the baby. Assure your child that it is safe and sure these days; the baby suffers no ill effects and the mother will be able to have another child. This type of birth gets its name from Julius Caesar, who is supposed to have been born this way.

LOOKING AHEAD TO MARRIAGE

The great process of reproduction begins with sexual intercourse, is followed by pregnancy, and ends in childbirth. Within this simple outline endless variation is possible, and endless opportunity for happiness. They are physical facts, but with many overtones of feeling that are among the richest rewards of life on earth. They may also be shadowed by the lifelong fears that people carry with them. But with each baby born, the fresh start is assured, the high promise is renewed, the vitality of the human spirit continued.

The age at which young people marry and discover these things for themselves—as they must for them to have full value and meaning—varies widely. But whether they marry in their teens or wait until later, they should not reach physical maturity ignorant of the way these three basic bodily processes occur. Information alone will not guarantee a successful sex life in marriage, but it will greatly improve the chances for sexual harmony, understanding, and happiness.

Like so much of the information in this book, however, the facts of sexual intercourse must be used wisely. What follows is perhaps told in more detail than some parents will wish to explain. Possibly the entire subject is one they would prefer to leave to a doctor or clergyman. Or you might want to let the child read it for himself. This, of course, is where the parent knows himself and his youngster best. Youngsters should not be kept in the dark if they want or need to know something, but this does not mean the parent must grit his teeth and struggle through an answer if he doesn't feel capable of handling the situation well. It is reasonable and honest enough to say, "Intercourse is a natural part of life and one you should know about. It's also very personal, and pretty complicated physically. I'm not sure I can explain it very well, but I'll be glad to have you talk with our doctor to get a clear explanation."

And a word of caution to parents who feel a discussion of intercourse with their children presents no problems: Wait to be asked. A young person, depending on his temperament or mood, may not welcome talk of these intimate matters now, just because you've been frank with him before or happen to think the time is right.

In short, getting outside help on a difficult issue does not make you a "bad" parent. And volunteering too much does not make you a "good" one.

"What happens in sexual intercourse?"

The entry of the male penis into the female vagina and the release of spermatozoa is sexual intercourse.

What is hard to describe, and what no one knows and understands until his time, is the mingling of feelings that overtakes the lovers as they embrace. It is—so to speak—a rainbow of emotion in which joy, tenderness, devotion, ardor all blend with the substance of each person's own unique personality to make the coming together of man and woman one of life's complete experiences.

The range of physical expression is equally wide. Almost every part of the body comes into play. Body temperature rises. Blood pressure rises, and the pulse rate increases. Breathing is faster. Nervous tension sets in.

Intercourse—or coitus—usually begins with kissing and caressing. In this the male usually leads, but, despite the old wives tales, there is no reason for the female to be inactive. The purpose of this wooing—or foreplay—is simply to kindle the desire of the partners and to bring them to a state of readiness at the same time. There is, therefore, no routine, no set plan or approach to be followed. Partners sensitive to each other's needs will catch the mood of each experience and act accordingly. Foreplay may go on for some time, or, on occasion, be omitted.

In the male, readiness comes with the firm erection of the penis. Internally, three organs take part in preparing the semen. The testes provide the spermatozoa. The seminal vesicles and the prostate, a gland the size of a chestnut which lies at the base of the bladder, produce a secretion that mixes with the sperm cells and carries them out. The seminal vesicles also store this fluid.

In the female, the vulva—the external lips leading to the vagina —swell in response to touch. The muscles of the vagina relax to permit entry of the penis. The clitoris, a small, highly sensitive organ just inside and at the apex of the vulva, becomes erect. Two small glands—Bartholin's glands—release a slippery fluid that lubricates the vaginal channel to make the entrance of the penis easier.

The usual position for intercourse in the western world is face-to-face. The female lies on her back, with her legs spread and knees drawn up. The male lies on top of her, supporting the weight of his upper body on hands or elbows.

When each is ready, the male inserts his penis into the vagina. Then, in a series of what are called copulatory movements, he moves it back and forth, penetrating and partially withdrawing. The female responds with a similar back-and-forth motion of the hips.

The pressure of the penis against the clitoris and other sensitive tissues usually brings the female to a climax or orgasm. Similarly, the friction of the penis against the vaginal walls brings the male to a climax, frequently before the female. In a series of jets, the seminal fluid is emitted through the penis into the female vagina. Of the millions of spermatozoa injected, only one will find, penetrate, and thus fertilize the waiting ovum.

At the end of intercourse, the body is satisfied and relaxes. The penis becomes limp, the female tissues subside. There is in both partners an afterglow of contentment and relaxation.

Item: Although this general description is accurate, there may be, as noted, many variations in procedure depending on the partners' desires.

Intercourse may go rapidly or slowly. Other positions may be used. There are no rules, except that it shall feel "right" and bring both partners to a satisfying climax together.

Item: No one can say how often or how long intercourse should take place. Again, if both partners are satisfied, there is no need to worry about what is "average." If there is a difference in feeling or performance, patience and co-operation are the best help. If there is a strong reluctance to discuss difficulties, get a doctor's help.

Item: Sex technique is not everything. The generosity of love must go with it.

"How do contraceptives work?"

There are a great many contraceptive methods in use today for the person who wishes them. (See page 86.) The choice should be made with a doctor's advice. Two kinds of these devices include one for men that fits over the penis and prevents the seminal fluid from escaping, and another for women that fits over the cervix, closing off the uterus so the male sperm cannot enter.

SEXUAL DISTURBANCES

There are several disturbances of sexual functioning which young people hear about and worry over for fear they may have them or get them. Each is explained in some detail below.

There are three things to be said about them. First, they are the exception, not the rule. Second, they are in most cases curable with professional help. And, most important, they are all too often the cause of unnecessary unhappiness to married couples who do not understand them. It is well for young people to remember that couples who blame each other for their troubles would do better to get expert medical advice. Either one may need treatment—along with sympathy, understanding, and support from the partner.

"What is sterility?"

Sterility, or infertility, is the inability to conceive a child. It is often assumed that the woman must be at fault, that she is unfortunately "barren." But since conception is a partnership, it is quite possible that the failure lies with the man. Merely being potent does not make it certain that a man is producing the necessary healthy sperm cells without which, of course, there can be no conception. Women, too, may have physical disorders which keep the process from being completed.

In other cases the trouble may be emotional. Being too anxious and eager to have a child may cause tensions and even prevent pregnancy.

Young couples should not jump to the conclusion that one or the other is infertile because there is no conception in the first few months of marriage. If a year has gone by, however, it would be best to have a physical examination—of both partners.

Sterility—and frigidity and impotence, too—are relative. They are rarely total and seldom permanent if properly treated.

"What is impotence?"

Impotence is the inability of a man to have an erection or to have one long enough to have successful sex relations, although he seems to desire intercourse. This, too, is a medical problem, probably with an emotional cause, but it can be treated and cured with professional help. It is not caused, as many people believe, by masturbation.

"What is frigidity?"

This term is often used carelessly and unfairly to mean a woman who is "cold" in sex relations. If she does not seem to enjoy or share fully in intercourse, if she is tense, or does not respond eagerly, she is supposed to be "frigid." Young people may even think that a girl who does not pet is "frigid."

Actually, frigidity might be defined as an emotional block that prevents a physical sexual expression, including orgasm (or climax), however much that person may consciously desire to respond to her mate in intercourse.

Stated simply, this means a woman because of some unconscious fear or disturbance may suffer an inability to want sex relations, even when she wishes to respond ardently.

Basically, the sex act is most satisfying when both partners can co-operate to give pleasure to each other. This takes sympathy, consideration, awareness—and patience.

Men, too, may be frigid. Their lack of desire may not prevent them from having intercourse. They may in fact be quite virile. But their interest is slight and infrequent. This may have a physical cause, such as a lack of hormones or vitamins. But in most cases it is probably emotional, as in the female. In either case, a doctor should be consulted.

PROBLEMS

Unfortunately, natural human sexual functions are sometimes perverted, which means they are put to uses other than the usual or intended one. Each person has his own attitude toward these activities or problems, but some care should be taken in the way they are impressed on young people. Since most youngsters know better than to involve themselves in this kind of trouble, there is no reason to add to the general, normal fears and interests of the age harsh threats and ugly warnings about the problems of the seamy side of life.

Specialists are pretty much agreed these days that sexual deviations—shifts away from the normal—are evidence of emotional disturbance, which is the result of failure of the sex impulse to follow the usual course in personality development. This need not make anyone more approving of them, but it may make him more understanding and less fearful.

"What is homosexuality?"

No longer is discussion of this subject taboo in the modern home, and it is well that we are finally facing up to the problem. True homosexuality is a preference in sex relations for a person of the same sex. Actually it is far more complex than this, with many degrees and many variations. Some homosexuality is "latent" only—a possibility, a tendency, but not openly expressed. Some homosexuals are also heterosexual—able to enjoy relations with the opposite sex. Quite often, too, homosexual activity may be a temporary situation resulting from emotional immaturity, which is later overcome, or from situations where there is no normal contact with the opposite sex.

"How do people become homosexuals?"

There are a number of theories but no certain proved one for the parent to pass along to his child. It does not seem to be a physical or glandular disturbance. It does not seem to be inherited. The best scientific information today is that it is tied up with emotional and personality development.

"Can you tell if someone's a homosexual?"

Except for the people who parade their problem in public, you can't identify a homosexual on sight. The gentle or graceful boy next door is not necessarily a "fairy" or a "swish"; a tomboyish girl is not necessarily a "Lesbian." Nor does a boy's skill at football or a girl's extreme femininity guarantee that they are immune to the problem.

"Could I become a homosexual?"

It is not very likely. Doctors know that every woman has some masculinity in her nature, just as every man has some femininity in his. This is called "bisexuality."

In adolescence, when sexual instincts are strong and adult sex relationships haven't yet formed, these tendencies may lead to "crushes" on members of the same sex. Sometimes a sexual episode may occur and an adolescent will fear that he has become a homosexual. Doctors do not take so harsh a view. The problem is a complicated one. Adolescent crushes, because they come at a time when emotional development is still in flux, are usually brief, and only a temporary substitute for heterosexual experience. Crushes are not considered serious evidence of homosexuality.

A parent who sees his own youngster in the course of such a friendship can usually sense when there is any abnormality present—usually, but not always. Speak frankly to your child and warn him, if you wish. But be very sure of yourself. The average teen-age crush does not have homosexual consequences, and may, in fact, be a constructive personal relationship. Parents can do harm by offering exaggerated and unnecessary warnings.

There is no reason, however, to hide the subject of homosexuality in mystery or evasion. Girls and boys both will learn, from their own observation, through chance gossip, from newspapers and books, of the existence of abnormal relationships. They will be less frightened and anxious about these aspects of man's sexual behavior if they receive sound knowledge and guidance from you.

"Is homosexuality curable?"

Some teen-agers may know of, or be approached by, a homosexual and will wonder if there isn't something that can be done for this unfortunate person. Since there are so many degrees and variations in homosexuality, and since the exact cause it not known and varies from individual to individual, there is no single "cure." This much is known: Homosexuals have been cured, but the homosexual person must want to change. Many individuals have temporary homosexual experience, and later move on to normal relations with the opposite sex.

"What is prostitution?"

This is the age-old, world-wide practice of providing sex relations for a price. Depending on the times and on society's standards, it has been openly permitted or sternly prohibited.

The point for young people—young men especially—is a simple one. No matter how much the gang may scoff, human sex relations should involve love. This is what makes them wonderful, what makes them the source of one of the deepest, most personal feelings a human being can have.

"Love" from a stranger is, in fact, no love at all. Despite the legend, sex relations with a prostitute contribute nothing to a young man's preparation for marriage. Despite the legend, prostitutes do not have hearts of gold, but are rather more likely to be tragic—and frigid—people. And they are certainly a prime source of venereal disease.

"What are venereal diseases?"

They are diseases usually contracted through sex relations with an infected person, man or woman. The two principal venereal diseases are gonorrhea and syphilis. (The word venereal comes from Venus, Goddess of Love, and the noun venery, meaning sexual intercourse.) Gonorrhea is a local infection which attacks the sex organs and urinary tract. Syphilis is a general and far more serious infection which can spread throughout the body by way of the blood stream. Both may be passed on to a fetus by an infected mother.

Both are curable in their early stages with various antibiotic "wonder drugs"—gonorrhea quickly, syphilis more slowly.

"What is an abortion?"

This has commonly come to mean the voluntary removal of a baby from the uterus—the destruction of a life that has started. It is illegal unless two or more doctors agree it is necessary to save the health of the mother.

Illegal abortions usually are attempts to end unwanted pregnancies. They must necessarily be performed outside a hospital by untrained or ill-equipped people and are quite dangerous, aside from the fact that they are cruel mental experiences.

Abortions may also be brought on by drugs or by physical

efforts of the woman herself. Both of these methods are extremely dangerous.

The main thing for young people to know about abortion is that it is a desperate solution to a difficult but not hopeless problem. A women, even if her pregnancy is unfortunate or accidental, usually feels a strong natural reluctance to get rid of her baby. When she does want to do so, it must mean that she is filled with tremendous fear, guilt, and loneliness.

Parents will have to decide for themselves how they would act if their daughter were about to be an unwed mother. There are many agencies ready and willing to help without asking questions or placing blame.

Any unmarried girl who is pregnant and cannot turn to her family for help and sympathetic understanding should place herself under a doctor's care and get from him the local clinics and organizations that can help her solve the problem of bearing, caring for, or adoption of her baby.

FOR THE PARENT

What is adolescence? First, adolescence is a physical fact that must be faced and accepted. The word itself comes from the Latin, meaning "to grow up." At the end of adolescence, however childish the personality which may live in it, the body is mature. Yet for a process so normal it often brings with it much anguish and grief. Both boys and girls may be anxious about, or distressed by, the bodily changes they experience. Frequently, their sensitivity is a symptom of a deeper concern about their own abilities in the face of adult responsibilities. They may wonder whether they can fill the male or female sexual role the changes are preparing them for. This is not meant in a narrow sense. Young people are not necessarily afraid of becoming fathers or mothers. But they wonder, sometimes uneasily, about the full range of activities and feelings that are involved in being manly or womanly.

In adolescence, therefore, you will first want your youngster to understand and accept comfortably the changes in his body.

What is the meaning of masculinity and femininity? You'll also want him (or her) to feel pride and ease in being masculine (or feminine) and to be able to regard his sex as a normal expression of the life he will lead as an adult.

While many of the customs, habits, and experiences of childhood mark the basic differences between the sexes, it is not until adolescence that these differences are solidified into lifelong personality patterns.

These patterns are more than just differences in body structure or dress. They have to do with feeling like a woman or a man. A girl cannot learn this only from other women, or a boy from other men. To be and feel feminine a girl must have male admiration and approval. A boy's masculinity depends in the same way on getting feminine love and approval.

This is not merely physical attraction, or a mating urge. It is sexual interest in a complete sense. It is the feeling that each sex has a unique part in life and a view of it which, when joined and shared with the other, gives each partner a greater sense of worth and completeness.

This may sound complicated. It is. But it develops in everyday ways. It comes from each sex working and playing with the other. It comes from boys and girls learning about and finding pleasure and satisfaction in their likenesses and in their differences.

How do we learn independence? Achieving independence as an individual able to stand on his own feet is another of the basic tasks of growing up that comes to a climax in adolescence. As you have seen in earlier chapters, almost every effort a child makes is aimed at equipping and preparing himself to choose his own way.

In adolescence, the choices become quite difficult. On any given subject there are many opinions to be considered. There are those of friends, who shape the standards and attitudes of the group the young person plays and works with most. There are those of parents, which seem less important now and often out of step with youthful views but still carry the great weight of age and of habit. For however rebellious they seem, adolescents dislike going against parents' wishes. Finally, and perhaps different from all the others, there are those of the young person himself. While he may be inexperienced and uncertain, he is strongly aware of his own hopes, fears, and wants. With any kind of encouragement he will try desperately hard to take responsibility for being and acting like himself.

Out of this will come first confidence, then respect. Having respect for himself, he can begin to show respect for the feelings of other people. And from such interest and sympathy grows love.

What is the adolescent's sexual development? The bodily changes that bring on physical maturity are accompanied by strong sex feelings and urges. While this is quite natural, it does not keep youngsters from being troubled by them. How much sex education a boy or girl has had earlier will have something to do with how much worry or anxiety he feels, but it is not the whole or only answer.

As far as we know, several things are going on inside the teenager that worry him at this time. First are his—or her—physical changes. These are dramatic and plain to see, and because they cannot be helped but just happen, they often make the youngster feel strange. Boys and girls are also very conscious of being like or unlike their friends. If they develop faster or slower or differently than their age-mates they fret. The only comfort parents can give is to point out that every person grows and changes at his own rate. And, generally speaking, that is the "right," the "normal" rate for him to grow.

Also a concern is the mere fact of having new, mature sexual capacities. Teen-agers wonder how and when and if they should use them. They joke boldly or nervously about them. They are tempted to pet, to have intercourse, to fall in love, and many of them do. For these are the new, exciting privileges of the physical coming of age. Yet they also realize that many of these activities —and their results—are forbidden or disapproved by their parents and the community.

The new development of their physical equipment, which has come upon them unasked for, opens up a whole new area of activities and relationships, all of them requiring hard choices and decisions.

A boy may feel he would like to have intercourse with a girl. He realizes he is mature enough to do so, yet he knows he shouldn't. He should wait till he is married. But that may be several years ahead. Perhaps he should limit himself to petting. But how much? Could he stop himself in time? And anyway, is he sure any girl will let him? And what will the boys say if he does? Or if he doesn't? And when, in fact, he finally has a chance to prove himself a male, will he be "all right?" The lack of clear-cut answers to these vexing problems raises anxiety.

Girls face similar problems. Generally, they mature a year or two earlier than boys and must wait impatiently for young males who will respond to their femininity. Or they find that they are attractive to boys who are older, more experienced, and only too eager to respond. This can be frightening and difficult for a young girl to handle. Girls, too, wonder how much they should pet and whether to have intercourse—and what would happen if they should become pregnant. There is much to think about.

Of course, in time, most youngsters work out some kind of solution to these problems. They may not be perfect answers. How could they be? But through trial and experiment, through making mistakes and learning from them, and through comparing notes with friends, they gain a new measure of wisdom and experience to carry them into adult maturity.

What should the teen-ager know about the male and female sexual systems? Every teen-ager, if he does not already know, should be told about the male and female sexual structure. It's unlikely that any youngster these days can reach the teens without finding out these facts somewhere along the way. But parents who for one reason or another have not made sex information a part of their youngster's growing up should nevertheless try to see that he has a clear understanding of these basic facts to help him through the problems of adolescence.

What should they know of the emotional aspect of sex? By the teen years youngsters are quite able to understand about the emotions—the feelings—that accompany the physical aspects of sex. Nature has seen to it that men and women are attracted to each other in order to reproduce themselves. Our society insists that this should not be a matter of chance or convenience, but that a man and women shall choose each other with care and join together, presumably for life, through marriage. This brings in the element of feeling and of love. Man and wife are attracted to each other as persons. They find worth and value in each other. They want to give each other happiness and are willing to share the other's unhappiness. And they want children to whom they can pass on the best hopes and feelings that are in them.

Sexual intercourse is at once the culmination and symbol of this kind of complete union. And it's a very important one. Many parents still suggest that the really meaningful aspects of life and love are mental or spiritual and that the physical element is a kind of afterthought, necessary perhaps, but not very. This just isn't true. All parts of our nature and our being need to express themselves and blend harmoniously together to create the wholeness and completeness of a truly happy marriage.

The teen-ager will be glad to hear this. The age is a romantic one, and one which seeks to express itself in many ways. It will do your boy or girl no harm to feel that a variety of feeling is all to the good.

One caution: Be as honest and realistic about these emotions as you can. Many parents tend to go to extremes. Either they draw an impossibly idealistic picture of a man's pure love for a good woman, or they take grim pleasure in warning young folks that life is full of troubles. Neither, of course, is quite true and no one knows it better than your children. They have seen that your own performance has often been less than noble, and they know that for all the ups and downs in their lives things could have been much worse.

Take the best elements of the youngster's romantic feelings—the wish to do wonderful favors for the loved one, to be true, gallant or gracious, wise, humorous and gay—as illustrations of what you mean by shared feeling. And for leavening, add from your own family experience examples of shared difficulties which also increased your feeling of closeness and affection for husband or wife. All of these examples, touching as they do on the youngster's experience, too, will give him a picture of the reality of mature emotions.

Won't they be promiscuous if I don't clamp down? No, they won't. Promiscuity in an adolescent who has been reared in a home where sex standards are discriminating is usually a sign of imbalance and will assert itself whether you are stern or lenient. However, the broader a youngster's knowledge of sex, the less likely he is to behave loosely and foolishly, the more likely to learn how to live with this element of himself. Clamping down is no way to help the search for understanding.

The promiscuous youngster is not a happy person. He, or she, is seeking through sex the admiration and approval that cannot be found at home or inside himself. It is, of course, a self-defeating effort. For being sexy, while it may attract attention, does not really reflect the complete personality, which is the basis upon which people usually make lasting relationships.

Promiscuity in adolescence is a fairly serious problem in self-adjustment. Parents would do well to help their youngsters get professional guidance.

How can I help my youngster through adolescence? First of all, don't be a worrier, too. Teen-age problems do cause concern because they involve important aspects of life, and because they come only shortly before the time when the youngster must play the role of man and woman.

But worry suggests caution. "Take it easy." "Play it safe." "Don't take chances." "Stay out of harm's way." And these are, as it happens, the sure ways for a child to miss out on the experience he needs to learn the lessons of adolescence.

Try to give your child the freedom to find his own way through the many choices offered him. And try to respect the choices he makes. For despite his worries, he wants even more to be adult and to decide things for himself.

Don't expect him to be very talkative about his feelings, especially those in the area of sex. Usually, teen-agers keep these to themselves.

Get used to the idea, too, that he will spend many hours daydreaming. This is normal, too. It is one of the ways he figures out his feelings about things and people and looks ahead, in imagination, to the future that is rushing toward him.

What about outside help? Teachers, clergymen, a coach, a Girl or Boy Scout counselor may also have a big place in your teenager's life. Very often an admired person outside the family circle can help a youngster solve some of his problems, either by advice or by example. Parents are sometimes jealous of these relationships. Don't you be. These friends do not have the same emotional ties to your youngster that you do, and can often make attractive to him an idea he has fought against taking from you.

How do I seem to my teen-ager? Your child probably sees you pretty much as you see him: realistically in some respects, unrealistically in others.

He sees you as much older than he is, which of course, you are. Parents often forget what an age difference can mean. They forget that they are more conservative and less flexible in their ideas than they think they are. They often are not aware of how the years have treated them. Many mothers do not see how fully they have occupied themselves with housework and how they have forgotten how it feels to be young. Fathers don't realize that the fortunes or misfortunes of middle age have affected their habits and opinions.

All this, however, your child sees—and more. Adolescent girls and boys are very much aware of their mother as a feminine person. They watch closely her moods and attitudes and ways of behaving. They are devoted to her and critical of her. They are almost as sensitive to their fathers and to his reactions to them. They are deeply hurt by his disapproval, or worse, by a lack of interest in them.

Both boys and girls may have varying general views of their parents. They may not like their name, their nationality, background, their politics or religion, their language or habits of eating or dress. Sometimes they swing the other way and place an extravagant value on the parents' attractiveness and skills.

These criticisms may hurt you. But try to see them for what they are. In questioning the facts of his life, the teen-ager is looking for bases on which to make choices for himself. He is trying to sort out what he likes and dislikes in order to get a sharper picture of himself as a person. In time, of course, he will probably be far more generous and understanding, and be better able to take people—including his parents—as they are.

THE GOAL: LOVE

As parents, what we want to give our children most of all is the capacity to love. This we do first by loving them and by responding to their love for us as it takes form. Later, we must be ready to stand aside when they begin to turn their love to others outside the family group, and finally to the man or woman they choose to marry.

The most important thing we can do for our children is to set a good example in our own lives. Through the kind of family life we live, our young people learn that love is based on respect for another human being—a respect we can feel only if we first have it for ourselves.

Of this respect, sex is a basic and important part. From knowing the truth about it at each stage of development and understanding, we gain a feeling of ease with ourselves, a feeling of satisfaction in being what we are, a feeling of kindness toward other individuals. Perhaps none of us achieves the ideal. All of us make mistakes along the way that make us fearful and less than we might be. Yet love is optimistic. Love is hopeful. And the chance to achieve it is always with us. This is the truth we can pass on to our children.

IF YOU NEED HELP

If your child's problems are too complex for you to handle alone, you can often get help from trained people in your community. Such people usually can be found in the guidance department of the school, in a family service agency, child-guidance clinic, or public-health center. If you do not know about such services, the Community Welfare Council can tell you where to go. Or you might want to talk to your own physician or religious adviser or to a psychiatrist.

If you have no local source of information, write to the Family Service Association of America, 44 East 23rd Street, New York 10, N.Y.; the National Association for Mental Health, 10 Columbus Circle, New York 19, N.Y.; or your county or state mental health society.

READING LIST

The following books are suggested reading for those who wish more information. They are available from their publishers or from your local bookstores and libraries. Only the starred (*) titles can be ordered from The Child Study Association of America. For information about other CSAA books and pamphlets on this and related subjects, write to The Child Study Association of America, 9 East 89th Street, New York 28, N.Y.

For the Early School Age

A Baby Is Born—The Story of How Life Begins, by Milton I. Levine, M.D., and Jean H. Seligmann. Rev. ed. 1962, Golden Press, $1.99.

* *The Wonderful Story of How You Were Born,* by Sidonie M. Gruenberg, with a guide to parents for using the book. Rev. ed. 1959, Doubleday, $2.50.

For the Later School Years

The Wonder of Life, by Milton I. Levine, M.D., and Jean H. Seligmann. Rev. ed., Golden Press, $2.99.

A Story About You: The Facts You Want to Know About Sex. The Dutton Series on Sex Education, by Marion O. Lerrigo and Helen Southard in consultation with Milton J. E. Senn, M.D. E. P. Dutton, $2.50.

A Doctor Talks to 9-to-12-Year-Olds, by Marion O. Lerrigo and Michael A. Cassidy, M.D. Budlong, $1.50. Available only through Milex Corporation, 5915 Northwest Highway, Chicago 31, Illinois.

For Teen-agers

Love and the Facts of Life, by Evelyn Millis Duvall. Rev. ed. 1963, Association Press, $4.95; Popular Library, 35¢.

Human Growth, by Lester F. Beck. Harcourt, Brace & World, $3.50.

Life and Growth, by Alice V. Keliher. Appleton, $2.44.

What's Happening to Me? Sex Education for the Teen-Ager. The Dutton Series on Sex Education, by Marion O. Lerrigo and Helen Southard in consultation with Milton J. E. Senn, M.D. E. P. Dutton, $2.50.

Sex and the Adolescent, by Maxine Davis. Dial, $5.00; Perma-books, 50¢.

The Girl That You Marry, by James H. S. Bossard and Eleanor S. Boll. Macrae Smith, $3.25.

The Man that You Marry, by Eleanor S. Boll. Macrae Smith, $3.25.

Understanding Sex, by Lester A. Kirkendall. Science Research Associates, 50¢.

What Teen-Agers Want to Know, by Florence Levinsohn. Budlong, $1.50. Available only through Milex Corporation, 5915 Northwest Highway, Chicago 31, Illinois.

For Young Adults

Learning About Love: Sound Facts and Healthy Attitudes Toward Sex and Marriage. The Dutton Series on Sex Education, by Marion O. Lerrigo and Helen Southard in consultation with Milton J. E. Senn, M.D. E. P. Dutton, $2.50.

When You Marry, by Evelyn Millis Duvall and Reuben Hill. Association Press, $4.95.

For Parents and Other Adults

Sex Pleasures in Marriage, by Jerome and Julia Rainer. Messner, $4.95.

Parents' Privilege: How, When and What to Tell Your Child About Sex (for parents of children under 8). The Dutton Series on Sex Education, by Marion O. Lerrigo and Helen Southard in consultation with Milton J. E. Senn, M.D. E. P. Dutton, $2.50.

*Our Children Today, edited by Sidonie M Gruenberg and Staff of The Child Study Association of America. Viking Press, $3.95.

Sex Facts and Attitudes (for parents and group leaders). The Dutton Series on Sex Education, by Marion O. Lerrigo and Helen Southard in consultation with Milton J. E. Senn, M.D. E. P. Dutton, $2.50.

* *The Encyclopedia of Child Care and Guidance,* edited by Sidonie M. Gruenberg. Doubleday, $7.50.

The Happy Family, by John Levy, M.D. and Ruth Monroe. Alfred A. Knopf, $4.95.

Marriage in the Modern World, by Phillip Polatin, M.D. and Ellen C. Philtine. Lippincott, $3.95.

Helping Boys and Girls Understand Their Sex Roles, by Milton I. Levine, M.D., and Jean H. Seligmann. Science Research Associates, 50¢.

Facts Aren't Enough, published by National Education Association, 50¢.

INDEX TO QUESTIONS

PREADOLESCENCE
CHILDREN'S QUESTIONS

PARENTS' QUESTIONS

TEEN-AGERS
CHILDREN'S QUESTIONS

LOOKING AHEAD TO MARRIAGE

SEXUAL DISTURBANCES

PROBLEMS

PARENTS' QUESTIONS